Qualifications and Credit Framework (QCF)
LEVEL 4 DIPLOMA IN ACCOUNTING

TEXT

Option Paper:
Business Tax
FA 2011

July 2011 Edition

For assessments from 1 March 2012.

Third edition July 2011

ISBN 9781 4453 7874 9

(Previous ISBN 9780 7517 9740 4)

British Library Cataloguing-in-Publication Data
A catalogue record for this book is available from the British Library

Published by

BPP Learning Media Ltd
BPP House
Aldine Place
London
W12 8AA

www.bpp.com/learningmedia

Printed in the United Kingdom

Your learning materials, published by BPP Learning Media Ltd, are printed on paper sourced from sustainable, managed forests.

CONTENTS

Introduction		v
Assessment Strategy		vii
Study Guide		ix
Tax Tables		xiii
1	The Tax Framework	1
2	Capital allowances	9
3	Computing trading income	31
4	Taxing unincorporated businesses	49
5	Partnerships	63
6	Losses	79
7	National insurance	85
8	Self assessment for individuals	91
9	Computing taxable total profits	105
10	Computing corporation tax payable	117
11	Chargeable gains for companies	133
12	Share disposals by companies	145
13	Corporation tax losses	157
14	Self assessment for companies	167
15	Chargeable gains for individuals	177
16	Share disposal by individuals	187
17	Reliefs for chargeable gains	195
Answers to chapter tasks		213
Test your learning – answers		251
Index		277

BPP note: AAT have advised us assessments under FA 2010 and F(No.2)A 2010 will cease to be available from end May 2012. Assessments under FA 2011 will be available from 1 March 2012 until 31 March 2013. Please ensure you check the date you intend to sit your assessment to ensure you are using the correct material.

A NOTE ABOUT COPYRIGHT

Dear Customer

What does the little © mean and why does it matter?

Your market-leading BPP books, course materials and e-learning materials do not write and update themselves. People write them: on their own behalf or as employees of an organisation that invests in this activity. Copyright law protects their livelihoods. It does so by creating rights over the use of the content.

Breach of copyright is a form of theft – as well as being a criminal offence in some jurisdictions, it is potentially a serious breach of professional ethics.

With current technology, things might seem a bit hazy but, basically, without the express permission of BPP Learning Media:

- Photocopying our materials is a breach of copyright
- Scanning, ripcasting or conversion of our digital materials into different file formats, uploading them to facebook or emailing them to your friends is a breach of copyright

You can, of course, sell your books, in the form in which you have bought them – once you have finished with them. (Is this fair to your fellow students? We update for a reason.)

And what about outside the UK? BPP Learning Media strives to make our materials available at prices students can afford by local printing arrangements, pricing policies and partnerships which are clearly listed on our website. A tiny minority ignore this and indulge in criminal activity by illegally photocopying our material or supporting organisations that do. If they act illegally and unethically in one area, can you really trust them?

INTRODUCTION

Since July 2010 the AAT's assessments have fallen within the **Qualifications and Credit Framework** and most papers are now assessed by way of an on demand **computer based assessment**. BPP Learning Media has invested heavily to produce new groundbreaking market leading resources. In particular, our **online question banks** ensure that students are prepared for online testing by means of an online environment where tasks mimic the style of the AAT's assessment tasks.

The BPP range of resources comprises:

- **Texts**, covering all the knowledge and understanding needed by students, with numerous illustrations of 'how it works', practical examples and tasks for students to use to consolidate their learning. The majority of tasks within the texts have been written in an interactive style that reflects the style of the online tasks the AAT will set. Texts are available in our traditional paper format and, in addition, as E books which can be downloaded to your PC or laptop.
- **Question Banks**, including additional learning tasks plus the AAT's practice assessment and a number of other full practice assessments. Full answers to all tasks and assessments, prepared by BPP Learning Media Ltd, are included. Our question banks are provided **free of charge** in an online environment which mimics the AAT's testing environment. This enables you to familiarise yourself with the environment in which you will be tested
- **Passcards,** which are handy pocket sized revision tools designed to fit in a handbag or briefcase to enable students to revise anywhere at anytime. All major points are covered in the passcards which have been designed to assist you in consolidating knowledge
- **Workbooks,** which have been designed to cover the units that are assessed by way of project/case study. The workbooks contain many practical tasks to assist in the learning process and also a sample assessment or project to work through.
- **Lecturers' resources**, providing a further bank of tasks, answers and full practice assessments for classroom use, available separately only to lecturers whose colleges adopt BPP Learning Media material. The practice assessments within the lecturers' resources are available in both paper format and online in e format. What fantastic news: you can now give your students an online mock.

This Text for Business Tax has been written specifically to ensure comprehensive yet concise coverage of the AAT's learning outcomes and assessment criteria.

Each chapter contains:

- clear, step by step explanation of the topic
- logical progression and linking from one chapter to the next
- numerous illustrations of 'how it works'
- interactive tasks within the text of the chapter itself, with answers at the back of the book. In general, these tasks have been written in the interactive form that students will see in their real assessments
- test your learning questions of varying complexity, again with answers supplied at the back of the book. In general these test questions have been written in the interactive form that students will see in their real assessments

The emphasis in all tasks and test questions is on the practical application of the skills acquired.

If you have any comments about this book, please e-mail ambercottrell@bpp.com or write to Amber Cottrell, Publishing Manager, BPP Learning Media Ltd, BPP House, Aldine Place, London W12 8AA.

ASSESSMENT STRATEGY

Business Tax is the second of two tax assessments at Level 4.

The assessment is normally a two hour computer based assessment.

The Business Tax assessment consists of eighteen tasks, seven in Section 1 and eleven in Section 2.

Section 1 covers:

- Capital allowances
- Adjustment of profits

There are six objective tasks and one extended task.

Section 2 covers:

- Capital assets for both individuals and companies
- National insurance contributions
- Payment of tax for income tax, corporation tax and capital gains tax
- Penalties
- Tax returns

There are ten objective tasks and one extended task requiring a written response, or the completion of pages from given tax returns.

Competency

Learners will be required to demonstrate competence in both sections of the assessment. For the purpose of assessment the competency level for AAT assessment is set at 70 per cent. The level descriptor in the table below describes the ability and skills students at this level must successfully demonstrate to achieve competence.

<table>
<tr><td>QCF Level descriptor</td><td>
Summary

Achievement at level 4 reflects the ability to identify and use relevant understanding, methods and skills to complete tasks and address problems that are well defined but complex and non-routine. It includes taking responsibility for overall courses of action as well as exercising autonomy and judgement within fairly broad parameters. It also reflects understanding of different perspectives or approaches within an area of study or work.

Knowledge and understanding
■ Practical, theoretical or technical understanding to address problems that are well defined but complex and non routine
■ Analyse, interpret and evaluate relevant information and ideas
■ Be aware of the nature and approximate scope of the area of study or work
■ Have an informed awareness of different perspectives or approaches within the area of study or work

Application and action
■ Address problems that are complex and non routine while normally fairly well defined
■ Identify, adapt and use appropriate methods and skills
■ Initiate and use appropriate investigation to inform actions
■ Review the effectiveness and appropriateness of methods, actions and results

Autonomy and accountability
■ Take responsibility for courses of action, including, where relevant, responsibility for the work of others
■ Exercise autonomy and judgement within broad but generally well-defined parameters
</td></tr>
</table>

STUDY GUIDE

Business Tax

Introduction

For the purpose of assessment the Principles of Business Tax (Knowledge) and Calculating Business Tax (Skills) will be combined. Please read this document in conjunction with the standards for the unit.

The purpose of the unit

The general purpose of these units is to enable learners to understand the impact and significance of taxation on both incorporated and unincorporated businesses. As accounting technicians, learners will impact on the accounts and finances of various businesses, and as such, should appreciate how those impacts will affect the eventual tax liability that will need to be paid.

By studying the basic tax rules and legislation that affect incorporated and unincorporated businesses, learners will understand that decisions made one way will have tax implications, but decisions made another way will have none. This should ensure that learners will be of benefit to the business when tax implications are of reliance.

Learning objectives

On completion of these units the learner will be able to:

- demonstrate understanding of the information required to complete tax returns for sole traders, partnerships and incorporated businesses
- recognise trading profits, making adjustments and applying the current relevant legislation to enable them to accurately prepare the required computations to support the completion and submission of the tax returns to the statutory authorities

Learning outcomes

This unit consists of 6 learning outcomes. The learner will:

(1) Understand the impact of legislation and legislative changes.

(2) Understand tax law and its implications for unincorporated businesses.

(3) Understand tax law and its implications for incorporated businesses.

(4) Understand how to treat capital assets.

(5) Prepare the relevant pages of a tax return for an unincorporated business and accurately produce the computations to support this.

(6) Correctly complete corporation tax returns with all supporting computations for incorporated businesses.

Delivery guidance

General tax issues

This area underpins all the other specific taxation areas assessed within this unit. It should not be seen in isolation as, for instance, the Finance Act being assessed is relevant throughout the standards.

Capital allowances

Always a complex area, learners must ensure that they are fully conversant with this topic. Not only must learners know how to do the calculations for plant and machinery, they must be able to explain these rules to tax payers. Capital allowances as they apply to opening, continuing and closing businesses must also be understood.

The key differences between the capital allowance computations under income tax rules and corporate tax rules must be understood, in particular the effect of private usage of assets.

Unincorporated businesses

Badges of trade will feature when learners start to understand how to decide if a trade is being carried on. Learners will need to be able to consider various situations and scenarios, and apply the rules under the badges of trade to determine how HMRC would consider the situation in the light of trading.

Computation of trading profit, or loss, will be key, with learners needing to demonstrate understanding on the differences between capital and revenue expenses. The impact of private usage will also need to be understood. Once computed, learners will need to be able to apply the basis of assessment to the adjusted profits. This will be for opening, continuing and closing businesses. Overlap profits will need to be computed, but change of accounting date will not be assessed.

Where losses apply, only those rules for continuing businesses will need to be understood.

In relation to partnerships, there will be a maximum of three partners in any one scenario. Changes to partnerships will be assessed for changes to the partnership agreement and changes to the actual partners themselves.

Incorporated businesses

All aspects of computations leading to the 'taxable total profits' will be assessable. This will be for companies whose periods of account are less than, equal to, or longer than, twelve months. Relief of trading losses will also need to be understood.

Capital assets – individuals

Learners must appreciate who and what is taxable under this heading. The impact that relationships between connected persons have on disposal of capital assets needs to be understood.

Detailed computations can be expected on chargeable assets being disposed of, including enhancement expenditure and part disposals. Complications including shares are to be expected, including rights issues and bonus issues.

Reliefs applicable to individuals, including entrepreneurs' relief, rollover relief and gift relief, are assessable. However, exempt assets, such as principal private residence and chattels, are not. *(BPP note: the AAT has now said that chattels are examinable, please see the note below).*

Capital assets – companies

This is virtually the same as for the capital assets of individuals, but the only relief assessable is rollover. The actual computation of indexation allowance will not be needed as this will be given.

National insurance

This is only in relation to self employed persons. Therefore, only Class 2 and Class 4 will need to be understood.

Payment of tax – income tax

A deep understanding of the payments on account system is expected, including when payments are due and how to pay them.

Payment of tax – corporation tax

All aspects of the payment of corporation tax are expected to be understood. The impact of short periods of account, 31 March straddle and associated companies are all expected. In addition, learners must be able to state the due dates of payment, whether a large company or small. Complex issues around instalments will not be expected, but the principles and being able to identify the right dates for any year end is necessary.

Payment of tax – capital gains

Learners should be able to apply the relevant rate of tax for capital gains, after taking into account all related reliefs, including the annual exempt amount.

Penalties

Learners need to understand the rules for penalties, surcharges and interest as they apply to payment of tax, posting of tax returns and filing of incorrect tax returns. No detailed computations will be needed, especially on daily calculations of interest, but the principles will need to be understood. This applies to income tax, corporation tax and capital gains tax.

Tax returns

There are three tax returns that are assessable: self employed, partnership supplementary pages; incorporated companies. These are expected to be completed with accuracy and completed in conjunction with the learner's own figures.

BPP Learning Media clarification with the AAT

BPP Learning Media has obtained clarification of a number of issues relating to the syllabus from the AAT including the following:

BPP query	AAT response
Please clarify whether the CGT chattels rules are examinable for individuals as well as companies – there is a conflict between the general and the detailed guidance on this point.	Chattels is examinable for both individuals and companies.
Are the supplementary partnership pages, which have been added to the list of tax forms to be completed, the short Partnership pages (S104S) completed by individual taxpayers?	This refers to SA800, the Partnership Tax Return. The partnership statement (short) pages at the end of this form needs also to be covered.

TAX TABLES

Capital allowances

Writing down allowance	
Plant and machinery	20%
Annual investment allowance	£100,000
First year allowance	
Energy saving and water efficient plant	100%
Motor cars	
CO_2 emissions up to 110g/km (low emission cars)	100%
CO_2 emissions between 111g/km and 160g/km	20%
CO_2 emissions over 160g/km	10%

National insurance contributions

Class 2 contributions	£2.50 per week
Small earnings exception	£5,315 per year
Class 4 contributions	
Main rate	9%
Additional rate	2%
Lower profits limit	£7,225
Upper profits limit	£42,475

Corporation tax

Financial year	2011	2010
Small profits rate	20%	21%
Lower limit	300,000	300,000
Upper limit	1,500,000	1,500,000
Standard fraction	3/200	7/400
Main rate	26%	28%

Formula: Fraction × (U – A) × N/A

Capital gains tax

Rate of tax

Standard rate	18%
Higher rate (applicable over £35,000)	28%
Entrepreneurs' relief rate	10%
Annual exempt amount	£10,600
Entrepreneurs' relief	
Lifetime limit	£10,000,000

chapter 1: THE TAX FRAMEWORK

chapter coverage

In this opening chapter we will consider the various methods through which a business can be operated. We then see that the tax law governing businesses is included in both legislation and a body of law known as case law.

Finally, we briefly consider how to calculate an individual's income tax liability. You may need to be aware of this when dealing with business losses.

The topics that we shall cover are:

- Methods of operating a business
- Relevant legislation and guidance from HMRC
- Calculating an individual's income tax liability

METHODS OF OPERATING A BUSINESS

A person wishing to operate a business could do so:

(a) As a sole trader (ie a self employed individual), or
(b) in partnership with other self employed individuals, or
(c) through a limited company

Business taxes

Sole traders and partnerships are unincorporated businesses. This means that there is no legal separation between the individual(s) carrying on the business and the business itself. As a result the individual(s) concerned must pay income tax on any income arising from the business and capital gains tax on any gains arising on the disposal of business assets. As a general rule, income is a receipt that is expected to recur (such as business profits), and a gain arises on a one-off disposal of a capital asset for a profit (eg the profit on the sale of a factory used in the business). Sole traders and partners must also pay National Insurance Contributions (NICs) on their business profits.

Companies are incorporated businesses. This means they are taxed as separate legal entities independently of their owners. Companies must pay corporation tax on their total profits. Total profits include income arising from all sources and gains arising on the disposal of any assets.

Payment and administration of tax

Both companies and individuals must submit a regular tax return and pay any tax due by the due date. The due dates for submitting returns and paying tax differ for individuals and companies and will be looked at in Chapters 8 and 14 of this Text.

RELEVANT LEGISLATION AND GUIDANCE FROM HMRC

Most of the rules governing the above taxes are laid down in various Acts of parliament. These Acts are collectively known as the Tax Legislation. The existing Acts may be amended each year in the annual Finance Act(s). This Text includes the provisions of the Finance Act 2011. Assessments will test the provisions of the FA 2011 from 1 March 2012.

To help taxpayers, HM Revenue and Customs (HMRC), which administers tax in the UK, publish a wide range of guidance material on how they interpret the various Acts. Much of this information can be found on HMRC's website www.hmrc.gov.uk. However, none of HMRC's guidance material has the force of law. Although you may like to have a look at this website, you should find all you need for assessment purposes within this Text.

Sometimes there may be a disagreement between HMRC and a taxpayer as to how a certain part of the tax legislation should be interpreted. In this case either the taxpayer or HMRC may take the case to court.

Cases decided by the court provide guidance on how legislation should be interpreted and collectively form a second source of tax law known as case law. You will not be expected to quote the names of decided cases in your assessment but you may need to know the principle decided in a case. Where relevant this will be mentioned within this Text.

CALCULATING AN INDIVIDUAL'S INCOME TAX LIABILITY

We now briefly consider how to calculate an individual's income tax liability. You may need to be aware of this when dealing with business losses later in this Text. However, detailed income tax computations are not assessed in Business Tax. You will deal with income tax computations if you study Personal Tax.

Components of income

As well as income from his business, an individual trader may receive various other types of income, such as bank and building society interest, rental income and/or dividends. These different types of income are referred to as 'components'.

These components may be non-savings income, savings income, or dividend income.

Savings income is interest (eg from a bank or building society). Dividend income is dividends received from companies. Non-savings income is any other type of income eg trading income, employment income and property income.

Total income, net income and taxable income

All of an individual's components of income must be added together to arrive at TOTAL INCOME. Some items, such as some trading losses, are deducted from total income to compute NET INCOME. In many cases total income and net income will be the same because there are no deductions to be made from total income. We therefore just show the amount of net income. Individuals below the age of 65 are entitled to a personal allowance and those aged 65 or above are entitled to an age allowance. The personal allowance or age allowance is deducted from net income to arrive at TAXABLE INCOME. The personal allowance or age allowance effectively represents an amount of income that an individual may receive tax free. Where an individual has net income in excess of £100,000 the personal allowance is reduced, so that individuals with net income in excess of £114,950 receive no personal allowance.

Task 1

An individual has the following gross income in 2011/12.

	£
Trading income	16,000
Building society interest	6,000
Dividends	8,750

His personal allowance is £7,475. His taxable income is:

£	23,275

Income tax liability

The income is taxed in the following order:

(a) non-savings income
(b) savings income
(c) dividend income

Non-savings income is taxed in three bands. Non-savings income up to £35,000 is taxed at 20%. This is called the basic rate band. Non-savings income above £35,000 up to £150,000 is taxed at 40%. This is called the higher rate band. Non-savings income above £150,000 is taxed at 50%. This is called the additional rate band.

There is a savings starting rate of 10% that applies on savings income up to £2,560. However, because non-savings income is taxed first, if the individual has non-savings income, this is set against the starting rate band first. Savings income that does not fall within the starting rate band but falls within the basic rate band is taxed at 20%. Savings income in the higher rate band is taxed at 40% and savings income in the additional rate band is taxed at 50%.

Lastly, tax dividend income. If dividend income falls within the basic rate band, it is taxed at 10%. If, however, the dividend income falls in the higher rate band it is taxed at 32.5% and if it falls in the additional rate band it is taxed at 42.5%.

HOW IT WORKS

Zoë has taxable income of £40,000. Of this £24,000 is non-savings income, £10,000 is interest and £6,000 is dividend income.

Zoë's income tax liability for 2011/12 is calculated as follows:

			£
Non savings income			
	£24,000	× 20%	4,800.00
Savings income			
	£10,000	× 20%	2,000.00
Dividend income			
	£1,000	× 10%	100.00
	£5,000	× 32.5%	1,625.00
	6,000		
Tax liability			8,525.00

Task 2

Mark has total taxable income of £50,000 for 2011/12. All of his income is non-savings income. Mark's income tax liability is:

£	13,000

35@ 20% = 7000
15@ 40% = 6000
13,000

HOW IT WORKS

Andreas has taxable income of £8,000. Of this, £2,000 is non-savings income and £6,000 is savings income.

His income tax liability for 2011/12 is calculated as follows:

			£
Non savings income			
	£2,000	× 20%	400.00
Savings income			
	£560	× 10%	56.00
	£5,440	× 20%	1,088.00
	£6,000		
Tax liability			1,544.00

Task 3

Jo has taxable income of £40,000. Of this, £1,500 is non-savings income, £30,000 is savings income and £8,500 is dividend income.

Jo's income tax liability for 2011/12 is:

£	8,169

1500 @ 20% = 300
1060 @ 10% = 106
28940 @ 20% = 5788
3500 @ 10% = 350
5000 @ 32.5% = 1625
8169

HOW IT WORKS

Clive has taxable income of £190,000. Of this £140,000 is non-savings income, £30,000 is interest and £20,000 is dividend income.

Clive's income tax liability for 2011/12 is calculated as follows:

			£
Non savings income			
	£35,000	× 20%	7,000.00
	£105,000	× 40%	42,000.00
	£140,000		
Savings income			
	£10,000	× 40%	4,000.00
	£20,000	× 50%	10,000.00
	£30,000		
Dividend income			
	£20,000	× 42.5%	8,500.00
Tax liability			71,500.00

Task 4

Sharon has total taxable income of £175,000 for 2011/12. Of this £120,000 is non-savings income and £55,000 is dividend income. Sharon's income tax liability is:

£	61,375

35,000 @ 20% = 7000
85,000 @ 40% = 34000
30,000 @ 32.5% = 9750
25,000 @ 42.5% = 10625
61375

CHAPTER OVERVIEW

- A business may be operated by a sole trader, partnership or company
- Individuals trading as sole traders or in partnerships pay income tax, capital gains tax and NICs
- Companies suffer corporation tax
- Companies and individuals must submit regular tax returns
- All of an individual's components of income are added together to arrive at total income
- Trading losses are deducted from total income to arrive at net income
- A personal allowance or age allowance is deducted from net income to arrive at taxable income
- Taxable income is taxed at one of six rates, depending on which rate band it falls into and the type of income it is

Keywords

Total income – is the total of an individual's components of income from all sources

Net income – is total income minus eg trading losses

Taxable income – is an individual's net income minus his personal allowance or age allowance

TEST YOUR LEARNING

Test 1

True/false: a company pays income tax on its total profits.

Test 2

All of an individual's components of income are added together to arrive at ____________________. Fill in the blank.

Test 3

Arun (aged 35) has the following gross income in 2011/12:

Non savings income	£25,000
Savings income	£12,000
Dividend income	£10,000

Arun's income tax liability for 2011/12 is:

£	

chapter 2: CAPITAL ALLOWANCES

chapter coverage

Capital allowances give tax relief to businesses who invest in capital assets. We start this chapter by thinking about the difference between revenue expenditure and capital expenditure.

However, as capital allowances are not automatically available on all assets acquired by a trader, we then learn when expenditure on plant and machinery qualifies for capital allowances. We then see how to calculate those allowances.

The topics that we shall cover are:

- Capital and revenue expenditure
- Expenditure qualifying for capital allowances
- Allowances on plant and machinery

CAPITAL AND REVENUE EXPENDITURE

In general, revenue expenditure is the day to day expenditure by a trader, for example on lighting, heating, stationery and wages. Capital expenditure relates to the acquisition or improvement of a capital asset such as machinery or a shop.

The importance of distinguishing between capital expenditure and revenue expenditure is that revenue (or income) expenditure is an allowable expense when computing trading income but capital expenditure is not. Instead there is a system of capital allowances that gives relief for tax purposes on some types of expenditure on capital assets as we will see in this chapter.

We investigate the distinction between revenue expenditure and capital expenditure further when we look at computing trading income later in this Text.

Task 1

For the following, tick if they are revenue or capital based.

	Revenue	Capital
Rent paid on premises	✓	
Purchase of machinery		✓
Repairs to machinery	✓	
Redecoration of premises	✓	

EXPENDITURE QUALIFYING FOR CAPITAL ALLOWANCES

Expenditure on plant and machinery qualifies for capital allowances. For this purpose machinery is given its ordinary everyday meaning. Plant, however, is harder to define.

The main description of PLANT is that plant is apparatus that performs a job in the business. Apparatus that is merely part of the setting of the business is not plant.

The following table gives examples of what is and what is not plant:

Items that are plant	Items that are not plant	Comments
Moveable office partitioning	Fixed office partitioning	Fixed partitioning is part of the setting in which a business is carried on. However, moveable partitioning performs a function in the trade and capital allowances are available on it.
Special display lighting in retail premises	General lighting used in retail premises	Special lighting performs a function in the trade so capital allowances are available on it
Decorative assets (eg lights, decor and murals) used in hotels etc where the function of those items is to create a certain ambience		

The following items also qualify as plant:

- Cars, vans, lorries etc
- Furniture
- Computers

ALLOWANCES ON PLANT AND MACHINERY

The main pool

Most expenditure on plant and machinery is put into a pool known as the main pool. This includes expenditure on cars with CO_2 emissions of 160g/km or less acquired on or after 6 April 2009 (1 April 2009 for companies). Capital allowances are claimed on the expenditure, as described in this chapter, and any balance of expenditure remaining in the pool after allowances are claimed, is carried forward to the next period.

Annual investment allowance

A business can claim an ANNUAL INVESTMENT ALLOWANCE (AIA) on the first £100,000 of expenditure in a 12 month PERIOD OF ACCOUNT on plant or machinery, other than cars. The period of account is the period for which the business prepares its accounts.

HOW IT WORKS

Keiran starts a business on 6 April 2011 and makes up his first set of accounts to 5 April 2012. He buys the following items of plants and machinery.

		£
12 April 2011	Office equipment	22,000
13 July 2011	Delivery van	35,000
1 August 2011	Car for salesman, CO_2 emissions 125g/km	14,000
2 February 2012	Machine for workshop	39,000

The maximum amount of the annual investment allowance that Keiran can claim is:

		£
12 April 2011	Office equipment	22,000
13 July 2011	Delivery van	35,000
2 February 2012	Machine for workshop	39,000
AIA for y/e 5 April 2012 (less than £100,000)		96,000

The AIA cannot be used against the cost of the car. Note that the AIA is available against the cost of the delivery van, however.

Task 2

Marcus has been trading for many years, making up accounts to 31 July each year. In the year to 31 December 2011 he buys the following items of plant and machinery:

		£
14 May 2011	Computer	2,000
12 July 2011	General lighting in showroom	1,000
12 September 2011	Office furniture	37,000
17 November 2011	Digger	65,000

(1) Tick for which of these items Marcus can claim the Annual Investment Allowance

	Claim	*Not claim*
Computer	☑	☐
General lighting in showroom	☐	☑
Office furniture	☑	☐
Digger	☑	☐

(2) The maximum AIA that Marcus can claim is:

£	100,000

First year allowance at the rate of 100%

A 100% first year allowance is available in the period in which expenditure is incurred on:

(a) Cars with CO_2 emissions not exceeding 110g/km (low emission cars) or electrically propelled

(b) Energy saving and water efficient plant

HOW IT WORKS

Ruby started business as a sole trader on 1 October 2010 and made up her first set of accounts to 30 September 2011.

In the year to 30 September 2011, Ruby bought the following assets:

9 January 2011	Plant	£30,000
10 August 2011	Machinery	£56,000
13 September 2011	Car (CO_2 emissions 105g/km)	£7,000

The capital allowances available to Ruby in the year to 30 September 2011 are:

	AIA	***FYA @ 100%***	***Main pool***	***Allowances***
	£	**£**	**£**	**£**
y/e 30 September 2011				
AIA only additions				
09.01.11 Plant	30,000			
10.08.11 Machinery	56,000			
AIA (max £100,000)	(86,000)			86,000
	0			
FYA @ 100% addition				
13.09.11 Low emission car		7,000		
FYA @ 100%		(7,000)		7,000
Balance to transfer				
to main pool	(0)		0	
C/f			0	
Capital allowances				93,000

Writing down allowance

A WRITING DOWN ALLOWANCE (WDA) is given on the main pool at the rate of 20% a year (on a reducing balance basis). The WDA is calculated on the value of pooled plant, after adding current period additions and taking out current period disposals (as explained shortly). The additions will include any expenditure that qualifies for AIA that is in excess of £100,000.

HOW IT WORKS

On 6 April 2011 Panikah has a balance on his main pool of plant and machinery of £28,000. In the year to 5 April 2012 he bought a car with CO_2 emissions of 130g/km for £10,000. He also sold a machine for £2,000. The capital allowances available for the year are:

	Main pool	*Allowances*
	£	
B/f	28,000	
Addition (no AIA on car)	10,000	
Less disposal	(2,000)	
	36,000	
WDA @ 20%	(7,200)	7,200
C/f	28,800	

Task 3

Nitin has a balance of £10,000 brought forward on 6 April 2011 on his main pool of plant and machinery. In the year to 5 April 2012 he bought a car with CO_2 emissions of 140g/km for £8,000 and disposed of an asset for £6,000.

Calculate the capital allowances available on the main pool.

HOW IT WORKS

Julia is a sole trader making up accounts to 5 October each year. At 5 October 2010, the value carried forward in her main pool is £20,000.

In the year to 5 October 2011, Julia bought the following assets:

1 December 2010	Machine	£90,000
12 February 2011	Van	£17,500
10 August 2011	Car for salesman (CO_2 emissions 135g/km)	£9,000

She disposed of plant on 15 June 2011 for £12,000.

The maximum capital allowances that Julia can claim for the year ended 5 October 2011 are:

	AIA	Main pool	Allowances
	£	£	£
Y/e 5 October 2011			
B/f		20,000	
AIA additions			
1.12.10 Machine	90,000		
12.02.11 Van	17,500		
	107,500		
AIA	(100,000)		100,000
	7,500		
Transfer to main pool	(7,500)	7,500	
Non AIA additions			
10.08.11 Car		9,000	
Disposal			
15.06.11 Plant		(12,000)	
		24,500	
WDA @ 20%		(4,900)	4,900
C/f	-	19,600	
Maximum capital allowances			104,900

Note the layout of this computation and the order in which the figures are entered. It is important to transfer the excess amount remaining after applying the AIA, to the pool as this excess is entitled to the normal WDA of 20%.

Task 4

Bernard is a sole trader making up accounts to 31 December each year. At 1 January 2011, the brought forward value on his main pool is £10,000.

In the year to 31 December 2011, Bernard bought the following assets:

10 July 2011	Machine	£73,000
15 November 2011	Lorry	£47,000

He made no disposals during the year.

Compute the maximum capital allowances claim that Bernard can make for the year ended 31 December 2011.

Disposals

As you have seen above, the most common disposal value at which assets are entered in a capital allowances computation is the sale proceeds. However, there is an overriding rule that the capital allowances disposal value cannot exceed the original purchase price of the asset. Try applying this rule in the following Task.

Task 5

On 6 April 2011, a sole trader had a balance on his main pool of £47,000. Plant that had cost £7,000 was sold for £14,000 on 1 August 2011. Calculate the maximum capital allowances available on this main pool for the year to 5 April 2012.

Periods that are not 12 months long

The annual investment allowance and the writing down allowance are adjusted by the fraction months/12:

(a) For unincorporated businesses where the period of account is longer or shorter than 12 months.

(b) For companies where the accounting period is shorter than 12 months (a company's accounting period for tax purposes is never longer than 12 months). Remember that we will be studying companies in detail later in this Text. We will see what is meant by an accounting period then.

The 100% first year allowance is not adjusted for periods of account shorter or longer than 12 months.

HOW IT WORKS

Melissa had a value brought forward on her main pool of plant and machinery on 1 April 2011 of £40,000.

She prepared accounts for the nine months to 31 December 2011.

Melissa's maximum capital allowances for this period, assuming there were no disposals or additions are computed as follows:

	£
B/f	40,000
WDA × 20% × 9/12	(6,000)
C/f	34,000

Melissa's maximum capital allowances for the period are £6,000.

In this example, the capital allowances would have been the same if this had related to a company, rather than Melissa.

Task 6

Gotaum had a tax written down value brought forward on his main pool of plant and machinery on 1 January 2012 of £20,000. He prepared accounts for the three months to 31 March 2012. During this period he bought a car with CO_2 emissions of 120g/km for £4,000.

Compute Gotaum's capital allowances, assuming there were no disposals in the period.

HOW IT WORKS

Oscar, a sole trader, makes up accounts for the 18 months to 31 December 2011. The brought forward value on his main pool on 1 July 2010 was £70,000. He bought the following assets:

10 July 2010	Plant	£70,000
10 October 2010	Car for salesman (CO_2 emissions 140g/km)	£11,000
12 August 2011	Plant	£95,000

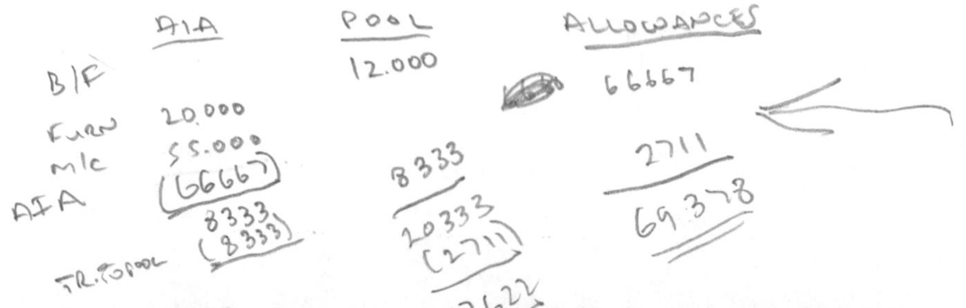

The capital allowances claim that Oscar can make for the period ended 31 December 2011 is calculated as follows:

	AIA	*Main pool*	*Allowances*
	£	£	£
P/E 31.12.11			
B/f		70,000	
AIA acquisition			
10.7.10 Plant	70,000		
12.8.11 Plant	95,000		
AIA £100,000 × 18/12	(150,000)		150,000
	15,000		
Transfer balance to pool	(15,000)	15,000	
Non AIA acquisition	***AIA***	***Main pool***	***Allowances***
10.10.10 Car		11,000	
		96,000	
WDA @ 20% x 18/12		(28,800)	28,800
C/f		67,200	
Allowances			178,800

Note: The AIA and WDA are scaled up for the eighteen month period. The same would not be true if this had related to a company, as the eighteen month period would be split into two accounting periods (a 12 month period and a six month period). We look at accounting periods for companies later in the Text.

Task 7

Marie has been trading for many years, making up her accounts to 30 April and made up accounts to 30 April 2011. The value of her main pool on 30 April 2011 was £12,000.

She then decided to make up her accounts to 31 December and made up accounts for the eight month period to 31 December 2011. In this period she bought the following assets:

14 June 2011	Office furniture	£20,000
15 August 2011	Machinery	£55,000

What is the capital allowances claim that Marie can make for the period ended 31 December 2011?

The cessation of a business

When a business stops trading, no AIA, WDAs or FYAs are given in the final period of account (unincorporated businesses) or accounting period (companies – see later in this Text).

Additions in the final period are added to the pool in the normal way. Similarly, any disposal proceeds (limited to cost) of assets sold in the final period are deducted from the balance of qualifying expenditure. If assets are not sold they are deemed to be disposed of on the final day of trading for their market value. This means that you must deduct the market value from the pool.

If, after the above adjustments, a balance of qualifying expenditure remains in the pool then a balancing allowance equal to this amount is given. The balancing allowance is deducted from taxable trading profits. If on the other hand the balance on the pool has become negative, a balancing charge equal to the negative amount is given. The balancing charge increases taxable trading profits.

HOW IT WORKS

The balance of expenditure on Raj's general pool of plant and machinery was £40,000 on 30 June 2011. Raj stopped trading on 31 December 2011. All assets in the main pool were sold on 31 December 2011 for £25,000.

Assuming that all assets sold were sold for less than cost, the balancing allowance or balancing charge arising in the final period is:

	£
B/f	40,000
Less disposal proceeds	(25,000)
	15,000
Balancing allowance	(15,000)

The balancing allowance is deducted in arriving at taxable trading profits.

Assets that are not included in the main pool

We have seen above how to compute capital allowances on the main pool of plant and machinery. However, some special items are not put into the main pool. A separate record of allowances must be kept for these assets. Assets that are not included in the main pool are:

(a) cars with CO_2 emissions in excess of 160g/km acquired on or after 6 April 2009 (1 April 2009 for companies);

(b) assets not wholly used for business purposes in unincorporated businesses (such as cars with private use by the proprietor);

(c) short-life assets for which an election has been made (see below).

We will look at each of these assets in turn.

Cars with CO_2 emissions in excess of 160g/km

Cars with CO_2 emissions in excess of 160g/km acquired on or after 6 April 2009 (1 April 2009 for companies) are put in a pool known as the SPECIAL RATE POOL. The WDA on the special rate pool is 10% for a 12 month period calculated on the pool balance (after any additions and disposals) at the end of the chargeable period.

HOW IT WORKS

Jason is a sole trader making up accounts to 30 November each year. The brought forward balance on his special rate pool on 1 December 2010 was £9,000. On 10 April 2011 Jason bought a car for £11,000 with CO_2 emissions of 165g/km. The car was used solely for business purposes.

The capital allowances available for the year to 30 November 2011 are:

	Special rate pool	***Allowances***
	£	£
y/e 30 November 2011		
B/f	9,000	
Addition	11,000	
	20,000	
WDA @ 10%	(2,000)	2,000
C/F	18,000	
Capital allowances		2,000

Task 8

Hermione commenced trading on 6 June 2011 and prepared her first accounts for the ten months to 5 April 2012. She bought a car with CO_2 emissions of 180 g/km for use in her business on 12 January 2012 for £18,000. Show the capital allowances available to Hermione in the ten months to 5 April 2012.

Assets used partly for private purposes

An asset (for example, a car) that is used partly for private purposes by a sole trader or a partner is never put in the main pool or special rate pool. You should put the asset in a pool of its own and then make all calculations on the full cost but claim only the business use proportion of the allowances.

An asset with some private use by an employee (not the business owner), however, suffers no restriction. The employee may be taxed on a benefit, so the business is entitled to full capital allowances on such assets. Similarly, there is never any private use restriction in a company's capital allowance computation (we look at companies later in this Text).

HOW IT WORKS

On 1 August 2011 a sole trader, who has been in business for many years, making up accounts to 31 December, buys a car with CO_2 emissions of 140g/km for £7,000. The private use proportion is 10%.

The capital allowances for the three years to 31 December 2013 are computed as follows:

	Private use car		***Allowances 90%***
	£		£
Y/e 31 December 2011			
Purchase price	7,000		
WDA 20% of £7,000 = £1,400	(1,400)	× 90%	1,260
	5,600		
Y/e 31 December 2012			
WDA @ 20%	(1,120)	× 90%	1,008
	4,480		
Y/e 31 December 2013			
WDA @ 20%	(896)	× 90%	806
C/f	3,584		

Note that full allowances are deducted in the private use asset column but the allowances (in the allowances column) to be deducted in computing taxable trading profits are restricted to the business proportion of the allowances.

If the car had emissions in excess of 160 g/km, the WDA would have been given at the rate of 10%.

Task 9

Pippa, a sole trader, bought a car with CO_2 emissions of 165g/km on 1 June 2011 for £20,000. She uses the car 75% for business purposes. Pippa makes up accounts to 5 April each year.

Show the capital allowances on the car for the year ended 5 April 2012.

Short life assets

A SHORT LIFE ASSET is an asset that a trader expects to dispose of within eight years of the end of the period of acquisition, if purchased on or after 1 April 2011. If the asset was purchased prior to 1 April 2011, it would have to be disposed of within four years of the end of the period of acquisition.

A trader can make a DEPOOLING ELECTION to keep such an asset in its own pool. The advantage of this is that a balancing allowance can be given when the asset is disposed of. For an unincorporated business, the time limit for electing is the 31 January that is 22 months after the end of the tax year in which the period of account of the expenditure ends. (For a company, it is two years after the end of the accounting period of the expenditure.)

If the asset is disposed of within eight years (or four years if purchased prior to 1 April 2011) of the end of the period of account or accounting period in which it was bought a balancing charge or allowance is made on its disposal. However, if the asset is not disposed of within this period it is transferred to the main pool at the end of that period. Short life asset treatment cannot be claimed for:

- Motor cars
- Plant used partly for private purposes

The AIA can be used against short life assets but it is more tax efficient to use it against expenditure that would fall into the main pool.

HOW IT WORKS

Nisar bought a computer on 1 March 2012 for £32,000 and elected for de-pooling. His accounting year end is 30 June. Calculate the balancing allowance due (if any) in the period of disposal on the computer if:

(a) The asset is scrapped for £3,500 in August 2019.
(b) The asset is scrapped for £1,200 in August 2020.

The brought forward value of the short life asset at 1 July 2019 is £5,369

(a)

	De-pooled asset
Year ended 30 June 2020	£
b/f – 1 July 2019	5,369
Disposal proceeds (Aug 2019)	(3,500)
Balancing allowance	1,869

(b) If the asset is still in use at 30 June 2020, a WDA of 20% × £5,369 = £1,074 would be claimable in year ended 30 June 2020. The unrelieved expenditure of £5,369 – £1,074 = £4,295 would be added to the main pool at the beginning of year ended 30 June 2021. The disposal proceeds of £1,200 would be deducted from the main pool in the year ended 30 June 2021 capital allowances computation. The balancing allowance would just form part of the balance to carry forward within the main pool.

Cars acquired before 6 April 2009 (1 April 2009 for companies)

Each car acquired before 6 April 2009 (1 April 2009 for companies) that cost more than £12,000 (sometimes called an 'expensive' car) is dealt with in its own pool. This means that a separate record of allowances and written down value is kept for each such car and when it is sold a balancing allowance or charge arises.

Expensive cars are eligible for writing down allowances at 20% regardless of their CO_2 emissions. However, the writing down allowance is the lower of 20% of the brought down value and £3,000 a year. In periods of account that are not 12 months long, the allowance is time apportioned.

Cars acquired before 6 April 2009 that cost £12,000 or less were pooled in the main pool, unless there was private use by a sole trader.

HOW IT WORKS

Dave is a sole trader making up accounts to 5 April each year. His business acquired two cars before 6 April 2009 which were used only for business purposes.

Car 1 cost £24,000 and had a brought forward value at 6 April 2011 of £18,000.

Car 2 cost £9,000. It is included in the main pool that had a brought forward value at 6 April 2011 of £33,000. It was sold on 10 March 2012 for £6,600.

There were no acquisition and no other disposals of assets in the year ended 5 April 2012.

The capital allowances Dave can claim for the year ended 5 April 2012 are:

	Main pool	***Car 1***	***Allowances***
	£	£	£
y/e 5 April 2012			
B/f	33,000	18,000	
Disposal			
10.3.12 Car 2	(6,600)		
	26,400		
WDA @ 20%	(5,280)		5,280
WDA lower of £18,000			
@ 20% and £3,000		(3,000)	3,000
C/f	21,120	15,000	
Capital allowances			8,280

A car with private use by a sole trader or partner is always dealt with its own pool, regardless of cost. Such cars acquired before 6 April 2009 are eligible for writing down allowances at the lower of 20% of the brought down value and £3,000 per year in the same way as cars without private use. However, only the business use proportion of the allowances is allowed as a deduction from trading profit, but the full allowance is deducted in calculating the car's value carried forward.

Task 10

Leonora is a sole trader making up accounts to 5 April each year. Her business acquired two cars before 6 April 2009.

The first car was a Nissan that cost £25,000 and had a brought down value at 6 April 2011 of £19,000. Leonora used the car 75% for business purposes and 25% for private purposes

The second car was a Ford that cost £15,000 and had a brought down value at 6 April 2011 of £9,600. It was used by an employee of Leonora 60% for business purposes and 40% for private purposes.

What are capital allowances that Leonora can claim for the year ended 5 April 2012 for these cars? £4170

	MAIN POOL	CAR 1 (75%)	CAR 2 (100%)	ALLOWANCES
B/F		19,000	9,600	
WDA 20% or £3000		(3000)	(1920)	2250 1920
C/F		16,000	7620	4170

CHAPTER OVERVIEW

- Assets that perform a function in the trade are generally plant. Assets that are part of the setting are not plant
- Most expenditure on plant and machinery goes into the main pool
- An annual investment allowance (AIA) of £100,000 is available on expenditure other than cars. The limit is prorated for periods of more or less than 12 months long.
- FYAs at 100% are available on low emission cars and energy and water saving plant
- There is a writing down allowance (WDA) of 20% on the balance of the main pool in a 12 month period
- WDAs are time apportioned in short or long periods
- FYAs are never time apportioned for short or long periods
- Private use assets by sole traders and partners have restricted capital allowances
- An election can be made to depool short life assets. If a depooled asset is not sold within eight years of the end of the period of acquisition, the value of the short life asset at the end of that period is transferred to the main pool
- Cars acquired before 6 April 2009 (1 April 2009 for companies) costing £12,000 or more are dealt with individually and have a WDA for a twelve month period of the lower of 20% of the brought forward value and £3,000.
- Cars acquired from 6 April 2009 (1 April 2009 for companies) onwards are dealt with according to their CO_2 emissions:

  Up to 110g/km – FYA at 100%

  111g/km to 160g/km – main pool with WDA of 20%

  Above 160g/km – special rate pool with WDA of 10%

Keywords

Plant – is apparatus that performs a function in the business. Apparatus that is merely part of the setting is not plant

An Annual Investment Allowance (AIA) – is available in a period in which expenditure is incurred on plant and machinery

A short life asset – is an asset that a trader expects to dispose of within eight years of the end of the period of acquisition

A depooling election – is an election not to put an asset into the main pool of plant and machinery

A Writing Down Allowance (WDA) – is a capital allowance of 20% per annum given on the main pool of plant and machinery

The period of account – is the period for which a business prepares its accounts

TEST YOUR LEARNING

Test 1

An item of plant is acquired for £2,000 and sold five years later for £3,200. The amount that will be deducted from the pool as proceeds when the disposal is made is:

£ 

Test 2

Nitin who prepares accounts to 30 June each year, had a balance on his main pool of £22,500 on 1 July 2010. In the year to 30 June 2011 he sold one asset and bought one asset as follows:

Disposal proceeds on sale on 1.5.11 (less than cost)	£7,800
Addition (eligible for AIA) 1.6.11	£123,000

The amount of capital allowances available for year ended 30 June 2011 is:

£ 

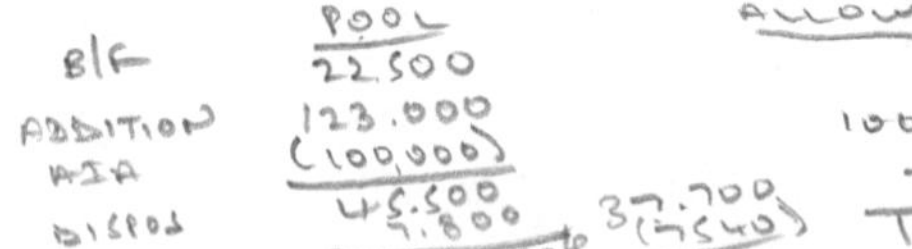

Test 3

An individual starts to trade on 1 July 2011, making up accounts to 31 December, and buys a car with CO_2 emission of 145g/km costing £18,000 on 15 July 2011. He buys energy saving plant costing £5,000 on 1 September 2011.

The capital allowances available in the first period of account to 31 December 2011 are:

£

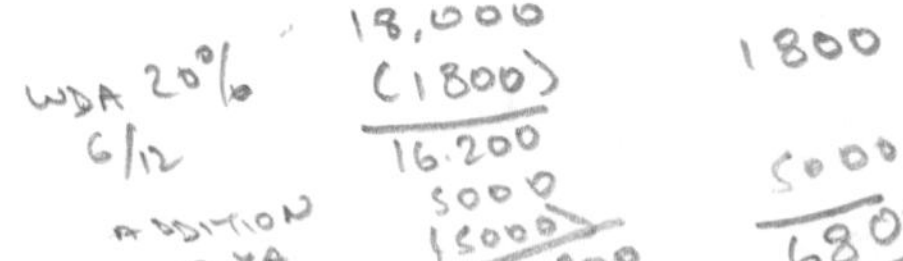

Test 4

Abdul ceased trading on 31 December 2011 drawing up his final accounts for the year to 31 December 2011.

The following facts are relevant:

Pool balance at 1.1.11	£12,500
Addition – 31.5.11	£20,000
Disposal proceeds (in total – proceeds not exceeding cost on any item) – 31.12.11	£18,300

True or false: there is a balancing charge of £8,300 arising for the year to 31 December 2011.

Test 5

Raj, a sole trader who makes up accounts to 30 April each year, buys a Volvo estate car with CO_2 emissions of 180g/km for £30,000 on 31 March 2012. 60% of his usage of the car is for business purposes.

The capital allowance available to Raj in respect of the car for y/e 30 April 2012 is

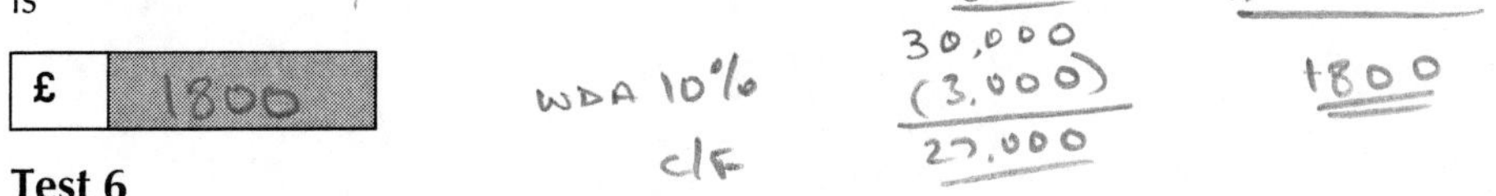

Test 6

Shauna is a sole trader making up accounts to 5 April. At 5 April 2011 the brought forward value of a car purchased in 2008 and used in her business was £19,000. It had CO_2 emissions of 170g/km.

The capital allowance that Shauna can claim on the car for y/e 5 April 2012 is:

A £3,800
B £3,000
C £1,900
D £1,500

chapter 3: COMPUTING TRADING INCOME

chapter coverage

We start this chapter by looking at the factors that HMRC consider when deciding whether a trade is being carried on. We then look at the detailed rules that determine how taxable trading profits are calculated.

The topics that we shall cover are:

- Is a trade being carried on?
- Capital and revenue expenditure
- Calculating trading profits
- Allowable and disallowable expenditure

IS A TRADE BEING CARRIED ON?

It is important to know whether an individual is trading or not. If he is trading, the profits of that trade are subject to income tax. However, if a trade is not being carried on, any profit arising on the sale of an item may be exempt from tax or it may be subject to capital gains tax.

For example, a person who buys and sells stamps may be trading as a stamp dealer. Alternatively, stamp collecting may be a hobby of that person. In this case he is probably not trading.

The badges of trade

It is necessary to look at a number of factors known as the BADGES OF TRADE when deciding if a trade is being carried on. The badges of trade each provide evidence as to whether a trade is being carried on. The overall weight of the evidence determines the final decision. The badges of trade are:

The subject matter

Some items are commonly held as an investment, for example, works of art and antiques. However, where the subject matter of a transaction is such that it would not normally be held as an investment (for example, 1,000,000 rolls of toilet paper), it is presumed that any profit on resale is a trading profit.

The frequency of transactions

A series of similar transactions indicates trading. Conversely, a single transaction is unlikely to be considered as a trade.

The length of ownership

The purchase and sale of items soon afterwards indicates trading. Conversely, if items are held for a long time before sale there is less likely to be a trade.

Supplementary work and marketing

If work is done to make an asset more marketable, or steps are taken to find purchasers, there is likely to be a trade. For example, when a group of accountants bought, blended and recasked a quantity of brandy they were held to be taxable on a trading profit when the brandy was later sold.

A profit motive

If an item is bought with the intention of selling it at a profit, a trade is likely to exist.

The way in which an asset was acquired

If goods are acquired unintentionally, for example, by gift or inheritance, their later sale is unlikely to constitute trading.

The taxpayer's intentions

Where objective criteria clearly indicate that a trade is being carried on, the taxpayer's intentions are irrelevant. If, however, a transaction (objectively) has a dual purpose, you should consider the taxpayer's intentions. An example of a transaction with a dual purpose is the acquisition of a site partly as premises from which to conduct another trade, and partly with a view to possible development and resale of the site.

HOW IT WORKS

Tim is employed by an NHS trust as a medical consultant. In his spare time he buys and sells stamps. Tim regards this as a hobby and his only intention in acquiring stamps is to add them to his collection.

Tim attends stamp auctions several times a year to acquire stamps. Stamps are usually bought in lots of several stamps. Most stamps he adds to his collection and does not intend to sell. Stamps that he does not want to add to his collection he sells soon after purchase, usually at a profit. Discuss whether or not Tim is trading with reference to the badges of trade.

We need to consider each of the badges of trade in turn:

The subject matter Many people collect stamps as a hobby whilst stamp dealers trade in the purchase and sale of stamps. In this case this badge of trade does not help to decide the issue either way.

The frequency of transactions Tim regularly attends stamp auctions to buy stamps and some stamps are sold soon after they are acquired. This frequency of purchasing and selling stamps may suggest that Tim trades in stamps.

The length of ownership The fact that most stamps are added to Tim's collection and not sold (ie held for a long period of time) suggests that Tim is not trading.

Supplementary work and marketing Tim does no supplementary work to the stamps and it is assumed that he does no marketing of the stamps he sells. As a result there is no indication that Tim is trading.

A profit motive Although Tim buys and immediately sells some stamps at a profit, his main intention is to find stamps for his collection. This indicates that he is not trading.

The manner in which stamps were acquired The fact that the stamps were bought rather than inherited or received by way of gift could indicate that Tim is trading.

It is the overall balance of the above evidence that determines whether a trade exists. On these facts it appears that Tim is not trading. Any profit on the sale of stamps could, however, be subject to capital gains tax.

CAPITAL AND REVENUE EXPENDITURE

You will remember that revenue expenditure is the day to day expenditure by a trader, for example on lighting, heating, stationery and wages. Capital expenditure relates to the acquisition or improvement of a capital asset such as machinery or a shop.

When we are calculating trade profits, the importance of distinguishing between capital expenditure and revenue expenditure is that revenue (or income) expenditure is an allowable expense when computing trading income. Conversely, capital expenditure is not, and so will be disallowed if it has been included in the income statement (profit and loss account) prepared by the trader. However, as we saw earlier in this Text, relief may be given for some types of capital expenditure through the capital allowances rules.

Task 1

Identify whether the following expenses are revenue or capital in nature by ticking the relevant box.

	Revenue	*Capital*
Paying employee wages	☑	☐
Paying rent for premises	☑	☐
Buying machinery	☐	☑
Buying a van	☐	☑
Building an extension to shop	☐	☑
Paying for repairs to car	☑	☐

Revenue expenditure

The distinction between capital and revenue expenditure can be a difficult one to make. The cost of repairing an asset is revenue expenditure but the cost of improving it is capital expenditure. The cost of repairs needed to put a newly acquired asset into a usable state is disallowable capital expenditure. However, the cost of repairs needed to remedy normal wear and tear on a newly acquired asset is allowable.

HOW IT WORKS

The cost of repairs needed to make a newly acquired ship seaworthy, before using it, is disallowable capital expenditure. However, if the ship had been seaworthy on acquisition the cost of making normal repairs would be allowable. This point was decided in a very famous case called *Law Shipping Co Ltd v CIR*.

You are not expected to remember case names for assessment purposes.

Task 2

A taxpayer bought a cinema that was usable on acquisition. However, the cinema was fairly dilapidated and various repairs were immediately carried out.

True or false: the repairs are disallowable, being a capital expense.

FALSE - REPAIR EXPENDITURE ALLOWABLE, AS THE CINEMA WAS USABLE ON ACQUISITION

CALCULATING TRADING PROFITS

If a taxpayer is trading it is important to be able to work out taxable trading profits.

The starting point is to take the net profit in the income statement prepared by the trader. The trader arrives at this profit by taking income and deducting various trading expenses. However, the trader is unlikely to follow tax rules in arriving at this profit as, for example, there are some costs for which HMRC will not allow a tax deduction even though the taxpayer quite legitimately deducts them for accounting purposes.

There are four types of adjustment that need to be made to accounting profit to arrive at taxable profit:

(1) Add back expenditure that has been deducted in the accounts but that is not allowable for tax purposes. This is called DISALLOWABLE (OR NON DEDUCTIBLE) EXPENDITURE. We will look at various types of disallowable expenditure below.

(2) Deduct income that has been included as income in the accounts but which is not taxable trading income. Examples are capital receipts (these may be subject to capital gains tax), income that is exempt from tax altogether or investment income (which is taxed separately to trading income).

(3) Deduct items that have not been deducted in the accounts but that tax law allows as a deduction from taxable trading profits. An example is capital allowances which you learned how to compute earlier in this Text.

(4) Add income that must be taxed as trading income but that is not included in the accounts. An example, is where the trader takes goods from his business for his own use. For tax purposes you should treat the trader as though he sold those goods for their market value. It is unlikely that the trader will have recorded this sale at market value in his accounts so an adjustment needs to be made.

Task 3

Pratish trades as a car mechanic. His most recent accounts show a profit of £38,000. In arriving at this figure he deducted entertaining expenses of £2,000 and depreciation of £4,000. These amounts are not allowable for tax purposes. Capital allowances of £3,500 are available for tax purposes.

Using the pro forma layout provided, calculate the taxable trading profit. The starting figure has already been entered for you.

	£
Net profit in accounts	38,000
ADD: ENTERTAINING EXPENSES	2000
DEPRECIATION	4000
	44,000
LESS: CAPITAL ALLOWANCES	(3500)
TAXABLE TRADING PROFIT	40,500

ALLOWABLE AND DISALLOWABLE EXPENDITURE

You may see allowable and disallowable expenditure referred to as deductible and non deductible expenditure. The two sets of terms are interchangeable.

The basic rule is that expenditure is allowable if it is revenue expenditure that is incurred WHOLLY AND EXCLUSIVELY FOR TRADE PURPOSES. If not, the expenditure is disallowable.

Wholly and exclusively for trade purposes

There is a case where a lady barrister incurred expenditure on black clothing to be worn in court. The expenditure was not deductible because it was not incurred exclusively for trade purposes. The expenditure had the dual purpose of allowing the barrister to be warmly and properly clad.

Strictly, expenditure incurred partly for private purposes and partly for business purposes has a dual purpose and is not deductible. However, HMRC sometimes allow taxpayers to apportion the expenditure between the part that is wholly for business purposes and therefore is deductible and the part that is wholly for private purposes and therefore not deductible.

HOW IT WORKS

A sole trader, who runs his business from home incurs £500 on heating and lighting bills. 30% of these bills relate to the business use of his house. £500 has been deducted in arriving at the accounts profit. How much should be added back in the calculation of taxable trading profits?

The 30% relating to business use is allowable. 70% × £500 = £350 must be added back to the accounts profit as disallowable expenditure.

Task 4

Raj deducts his total motor expenses of £600 in calculating his accounts profit. 60% of Raj's motoring is for business purposes and 40% is for private purposes.

The amount of the motoring expenses that must be added back to the accounts profit in calculating taxable trading profit is:

£	240

£600 × 40% = £240

Charitable donations

Donations to charity are not incidentally incurred in any trade. This means that they are not incurred for trade purposes and are therefore normally disallowable. However, where a donation is made to a small local charity, HMRC will allow the donation on the grounds that, in these circumstances, the donation is made to benefit the trade (through developing local goodwill etc).

Task 5

Norman, a greengrocer, deducts the following donations in computing his accounting profit:

£100 to Oxfam
£280 to a small local charity

The total amount of the donations that must be added back in computing taxable trading profits is:

£	100

The treatment of various other items

The table below details various types of allowable and disallowable expenditure. Both unincorporated businesses (sole traders and partnerships) and incorporated businesses (companies) may have trading income. The rules for computing taxable trading income for companies are slightly different to those for calculating taxable trading income for individuals/partnerships. Although this part of the Text is mainly concerned with unincorporated businesses, for completeness, we mention where the rules for companies differ at relevant points in the table below.

Allowable expenditure	Disallowable expenditure	Comments
	Fines and penalties	HMRC usually allow parking fines incurred in parking an employee's car whilst on the employer's business. Fines relating to the owner of the business are, however, never allowed. Similarly, a company would not be able to deduct fines relating to directors
Costs of registering trade marks and patents		
Incidental costs of obtaining loan finance		This deduction does not apply to companies because they get a deduction for the cost of borrowing in a different way. We look at companies later in this Text
	Depreciation or amortisation	In specific circumstances a company can deduct

Allowable expenditure	Disallowable expenditure	Comments
		these amounts, but this is outside the scope of Business Tax
	Any salary or interest paid to a sole trader or partner	
	The private proportion of any expenses incurred by a proprietor	The private proportion of an employee's expenses is, however, deductible
Impairment (bad) debts incurred in the course of a business. Specific provisions for impaired debts (see below)	General provisions for impaired debts (and other general provisions)	Loans to employees written off despite being specific are not allowable.
Patent and copyright royalties		Patent and copyright royalties paid for trade purposes are deductible
Staff entertaining	Non staff (eg customer) entertaining	
Gifts for employees Gifts to customers costing not more than £50 per donee per year if they carry a conspicuous advertisement for the business and are not food, drink, tobacco or vouchers exchangeable for such goods. Gifts to a small local charity if they benefit the trade	All other gifts including those made under the gift aid scheme	The Gift Aid scheme is a scheme under which tax relief is given on gifts. The scheme relevant to individuals is not assessable in Business Tax. Gift Aid in relation to companies is covered later in this Text.
Subscriptions to a professional or trade association	Political donations	Exceptionally, if it can be shown that political expenditure is incurred for the survival of the trade, then it is allowable
Legal and professional charges relating directly to the trade	Legal and professional charges relating to capital or non trading items	Deductible items include: ▪ charges incurred defending the taxpayer's title to non-current assets ▪ charges connected with an action for breach of contract ▪ expenses of the renewal (not the original grant) of a lease for less than 50 years

Allowable expenditure	Disallowable expenditure	Comments
		▪ charges for trade debt collection ▪ normal charges for preparing accounts and assisting with the self assessment of tax liabilities
Accountancy expenses arising from an enquiry	Accountancy expenses relating to specialist consultancy work	Expenses are not allowed if an enquiry reveals discrepancies and additional liabilities, that arise as a result of negligent or fraudulent conduct. Where, however, the enquiry results in no addition to profits, or an adjustment to the profits for the year of enquiry only and that assessment does not arise as a result of negligent or fraudulent conduct, the additional accountancy expenses are allowable
Interest on loans taken out for trade purposes	Interest on overdue tax	These rules are for unincorporated businesses. Companies have different rules for the cost of borrowing. We look at these later in this Text
Costs of seconding employees to charities or educational establishments		
Expenditure incurred in the seven years prior to the commencement of a trade		Provided expenditure is of a type that would have been allowed had the trade started. Treat as an expense on the first day of trading
Removal expenses (to new business premises)		Only if not an expansionary move
Travelling expenses on the trader's business	Travel from home to the trader's place of business	

Allowable expenditure	Disallowable expenditure	Comments
Redundancy payments		If the trade ceases, the limit on allowability is 3 × the statutory amount (in addition to the statutory amount)
	15% of leasing costs of car with CO_2 emissions in excess of 160g/km	

Impaired trade receivables (bad debts)

Only impairment debts incurred wholly and exclusively for the purposes of the trade are deductible for taxation purposes. Thus loans to employees written off are not deductible unless the business is that of making loans, or it can be shown that the write off was earnings paid out for the benefit of the trade.

A review of trade receivables may be carried out to assess their fair value, and any impairment debts written off. As a specific provision, this is an allowable expense and therefore no adjustment is needed.

Accounting rules are such that it is unlikely that any general provisions will be seen in practice. In the event that they do arise, increases or decreases in a general provision are not allowable and an adjustment is needed. Let's have a look at the following example of a impairment debts account:

HOW IT WORKS

IMPAIRMENT DEBTS ACCOUNT (BAD DEBTS)

The account below results in a credit to the income statement of £28. All the debts are trade debts. What adjustment should be made to net profit when calculating taxable trading profits?

2011	£	£	*2011*	£	£
			1 January		
Impairments written off			Provisions b/d		
J Jones	67		General	150	
A Smith	119		Specific	381	
		186			531
Provisions c/d					
General	207		Impairments recovered		90
Specific	200				
		407			
Income statement		28			
		621			621
			2012		
			1 January		
			Provisions b/d		407

Every adjustment shown is either taxable or tax deductible except for the increase in general provision from £150 to £207. Thus £57 is added to the accounts profit to arrive at taxable profit.

Task 6

A sole trader has an accounts profit of £180,000 after charging legal expenses as follows:

	£
Expenses relating to purchase of new offices	7,000
Expenses relating to employee service contracts	2,000
Expenses relating to the renewal of a 25 year lease	1,500

What amount of the above expenses must be added back in computing taxable trading profits?

A £7,000
B £9,000
C £10,500
D £8,500

Task 7

A sole trader charged the following expenses in computing his accounts profit:

	£
Fine for breach of Factories Act	1,000
Cost of specialist tax consultancy work	2,000
Redundancy payments	10,000
Salary for himself	15,000
Leasing cost of car (CO_2 emissions 170g/km)	3,000

The redundancy payments were made for trade purposes as a result of reorganisation of the business. The trade is continuing.

What is the total amount of the above expenses that must be added back in computing taxable trading profit?

A £17,450
B £16,000
C £18,450
D £11,450

Task 8

Sana runs her business from home. Sana has deducted all of her heating and lighting bills of £800 in computing her accounts profit. 30% of the heating and lighting bills relate to the business. The amount that must be added back in computing taxable trading profits is:

£	560

800 x 70% = 560

Task 9

The entertainment account of Green and Co showed:

	£
Staff tennis outing for 30 employees	1,800
2,000 tee shirts with firm's logo given to race runners	4,500
Advertising and sponsorship of an athletic event	2,000
Entertaining customers	7,300
Staff Christmas party (30 employees)	2,400

The amount that must be added back in arriving at taxable trading profits is:

£	7300

Task 10

Here is the income statement of S Pring, a trader.

	£	£
Gross operating profit		30,000
Rental income received		860
		30,860
Wages and salaries	7,000	
Rent and rates	2,000	
Depreciation	1,500	
Specific impairment debts written off	150	
Provision against a fall in the price of raw materials	5,000	
Entertainment expenses	750	
Patent royalties	1,200	
Bank interest	300	
Legal expenses on acquisition of new factory	250	
		(18,150)
Net profit		12,710

(a) Salaries include £500 paid to Mrs Pring who works full time in the business.

(b) No staff were entertained.

(c) The provision of £5,000 is a general provision charged because of an anticipated trade recession.

Using the pro forma layout provided, compute the taxable trading profit.

	£	£
NET PROFIT		12710
ADD: DEPRECIATION	1500	
PROVISION	5000	
ENTERTAINMENT	750	
LEGAL	250	
		7500
		20210
LESS: RENTAL INCOME		(860)
ADJUSTED TRADING PROFIT		19350

CHAPTER OVERVIEW

- The badges of trade indicate whether or not a trade is being carried on
- Revenue expenses are allowable expenses for computing taxable trading profits but capital expenses are not (unless relieved through capital allowances)
- The main disallowable items that you must add back in computing taxable trading profits are:
  - Entertaining (other than staff entertaining)
  - Depreciation (deduct capital allowances instead)
  - Increase in a general provisions
  - Fines
  - Legal fees relating to capital items
  - Wages or salary paid to a business owner
  - The private proportion of any expenses for a sole trader/partner
- Deduct non trading income/capital profits included in the accounts from the accounts profit to arrive at taxable trading profit

Keywords

Badges of trade – indicate whether or not a trade is being carried on

Disallowable expenditure – is expenditure that cannot be deducted in computing taxable trading profit

Expenditure wholly and exclusively for trade purposes – is expenditure that is incidental to the trade and that does not have a dual purpose

TEST YOUR LEARNING

Test 1

Which of the following expenses are allowable when computing taxable trading profits?

A Legal fees incurred on the acquisition of a factory to be used for trade purposes

B Heating for factory

C Legal fees incurred on pursuing trade receivables (debtors)

D Acquiring a machine to be used in the factory

Test 2

A sole trader incurs the following expenditure on entertaining and gifts

	£
Staff entertaining	700
50 Christmas food hampers given to customers	240
Entertaining customers	900
	1,840

How much of the above expenditure is allowable for tax purposes?

Test 3

For each of the following expenses, show whether they are allowable or disallowable by ticking the relevant boxes.

	Allowable	*Disallowable*
Parking fines incurred by the owner of the business	☐	☐
Parking fines incurred by an employee whilst on the employer's business	☐	☐
Legal costs incurred in relation to acquiring a 10 year lease of property for the first time	☐	☐
Legal costs incurred in relation to the renewal of a lease for 20 years.	☐	☐
Gifts of calendars to customers, costing £4 each and displaying an advertisement for the trade concerned	☐	☐
Gifts of bottles of whisky to customers, costing £12 each	☐	☐

Test 4

Herbert, a self-employed carpenter, makes various items of garden furniture for sale. He takes a bird table from stock and sets it up in his own garden. The cost of making the bird table amounts to £80, and Herbert would normally expect to achieve a mark-up of 20% on such goods.

What adjustment is to be made to the accounts for tax purposes, assuming Herbert has reflected this in the accounts by deducting the cost of the table?

A £80 must be deducted from the accounts profit
B £80 must be added back to the accounts profit
C £96 must be deducted from the accounts profit
D £96 must be added back to the accounts profit

Test 5

Set out below is the impairment debts account of Kingfisher, a sole trader:

IMPAIRMENT DEBTS

	£		£
		1.4.11	
Impairments written off		Provisions b/fwd	
		General	2,500
Specific trade receivables	1,495	Specific (trade)	1,875
		Impairments recovered specific trade receivables	275
31.3.12			
Provisions c/fwd			
General	1,800		
Specific (trade)	2,059	Income statement	704
	5,354		5,354

The amount that must be added to or deducted from Kingfisher's accounts profit to arrive at taxable trading profit is:

Test 6

Trude works from home as a self employed hairdresser. She incurs £450 on heating and lighting bills and this amount is deducted in her accounts. 20% of this expenditure relates to the business use of her home. How much of the expenditure is disallowable for tax purposes?

chapter 4: TAXING UNINCORPORATED BUSINESSES

chapter coverage 📖

Individuals must pay tax for tax years. In this chapter we see what is meant by a tax year and we learn how to arrive at the trading profits to be taxed in each tax year.

Finally, we look at the self employment tax pages which you may be required to complete in your assessment.

The topics that we shall cover are:

- Continuing businesses
- The start of trading
- The cessation of trading
- Overlap profits
- Self employment tax return page

CONTINUING BUSINESSES

Traders can produce their business accounts to any date in the year they choose. However, income tax is charged for tax years. This means that a mechanism is needed to link the taxable profits arising from a particular set of accounts to a tax year. This mechanism is known as the basis of assessment, and the period whose profits are assessed in a tax year is called the BASIS PERIOD.

The TAX YEAR, FISCAL YEAR or YEAR OF ASSESSMENT runs from 6 April in one year to 5 April in the next year. For example, 2011/12 runs from 6 April 2011 to 5 April 2012.

The basis of assessment for a continuing business is the 12 month period of account ending in a tax year. The profits resulting from those accounts are taxed in that tax year. This is known as the CURRENT YEAR BASIS OF ASSESSMENT.

HOW IT WORKS

If a trader prepares accounts to 30 April each year, the profits of the year to 30 April 2011 will be taxed in 2011/12. This is because the year to 30 April 2011 ends in 2011/12 (ie between the dates 6 April 2011 and 5 April 2012).

Task 1

Talet, a dressmaker, has been in business for many years and prepares accounts to 30 September each year. What is her basis period for 2011/12?

A 1 October 2011to 30 September 2012
B 1 April 2011 to 31 March 2012
C 1 October 2010 to 30 September 2011
D 6 April 2011 to 5 April 2012

THE START OF TRADING

On commencement of trade, the trader might not make up his first set of accounts for a 12 month period, therefore special rules are needed to find the basis period in the first three years of a new business. These rules always apply, even if the first set of accounts is for a 12 month period.

The first tax year

The tax year in which a trade starts is the first year in which profits will be taxed.

HOW IT WORKS

If a trade starts on 15 May 2011, the first tax year in which profits are taxed is 2011/12. This is the tax year into which the date of commencement falls.

This rule ensures that profits are taxed right from the start of a business.

The basis period for the first tax year runs from the date the trade starts to the next 5 April (or to the date of cessation if the trade does not continue until the end of the tax year). If accounts are not prepared to the end of the first tax year, you will need to time apportion taxable profits arising from one or more periods of account. For assessment purposes all time apportionment should be made on a monthly basis.

HOW IT WORKS

Sasha starts a trade on 1 December 2011. She prepares her first accounts for the ten months to 30 September 2012. The taxable profits arising as a result of these accounts are £60,000.

2011/12 is the tax year in which Sasha's trade starts, so the first year in which profits are taxed is 2011/12. The basis period for 2011/12 therefore, will run from 1 December 2011 to 5 April 2012. Taxable profits of £60,000 × 4/10 = £24,000 arise in this period and will be taxed in 2011/12.

The second tax year

Finding the basis period for the second tax year is tricky because there are three possibilities:

(a) If there is period of account that ends in the second tax year, but it is less than 12 months long, the basis period that must be used is the first 12 months of trading (ie increase the period to 12 months)

(b) If there is a period of account that ends in the second tax year, but is 12 months or longer, the basis period that must be used is the 12 months leading up the end of that period of account (ie reduce the period to 12 months, if necessary)

(c) If there is no period of account that ends in the second tax year, because the first period of account is a very long one which does not end until a date in the third tax year, the basis period that must be used for the second tax year is the year itself (from 6 April to 5 April).

Some students find the following flowchart helpful in determining the basis period for the second year:

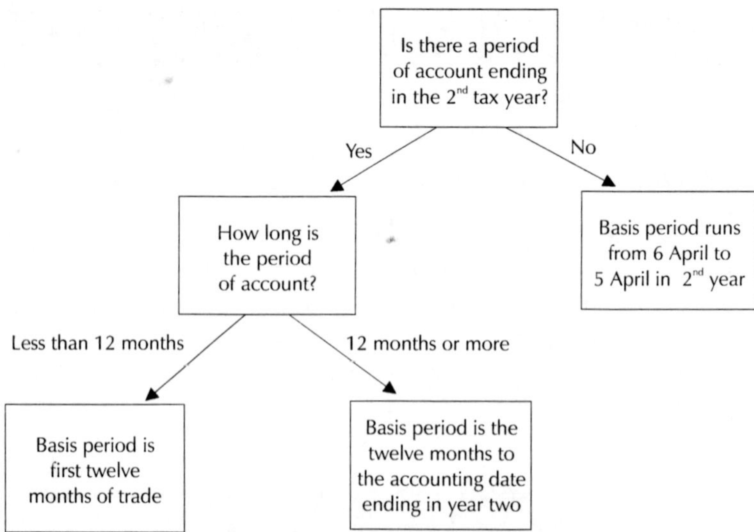

You can now use the flowchart to see if it helps you with the following examples:

HOW IT WORKS

Period of account ending in second year less than 12 months long

Janet starts trading on 1 July 2011. She prepares accounts for the ten months to 30 April 2012 and annually thereafter.

Janet's basis periods for the first two tax years of her business are:

Year	***Basis period***	
2011/12	1.7.11 – 5.4.12	(commencement to next 5 April)
2012/13	12 m to 30.06.12	(first 12 months)

HOW IT WORKS

Period of account ending in second year 12 months, or longer

John starts trading on 1 July 2011. He prepares accounts for the fifteen months to 30 September 2012.

John's basis periods for the first two tax years are:

Year	***Basis period***	
2011/12	1.7.11 – 5.4.12	(commencement to next 5 April)
2012/13	12 m to 30.9.12	(12 months ended in second tax year)

HOW IT WORKS

No period of account ending in second tax year

Abdul starts trading on 1 January 2011 and prepares accounts for the sixteen months to 30 April 2012.

Abdul's basis periods for the first two years are:

Year	***Basis period***	
2010/11	1.1.11 – 5.4.11	(commencement to next 5 April)
2011/12	6.4.11 – 5.4.12	(tax year)

Note that it was important to take care here and realise that the first tax year was 2010/11. This is because 1 January 2011 falls in 2010/11.

The third tax year

Finding the basis period in the third tax year is easier than the second year.

The basis period in the third year is always the 12 months to the end of the period of account ending in that year.

HOW IT WORKS

On 1 January 2011, Shamimma started trading. She prepares accounts to 31 December each year. What are the basis periods for the first three years of trading?

Solution

2010/11	1.1.11 – 5.4.11	(commencement to next 5 April)
2011/12	year to 31.12.11	(period of account ending in second year)
2012/13	year to 31.12.12	(12 month period ending in third year)

Now you can try a Task in which you must time apportion profits to the first three tax years. Remember that time apportionment for assessment purposes is done on a monthly basis.

Task 2

Kumar starts to trade on 1 June 2010, with the following results.

Period	*Profit*
	£
1.6.10 – 31.5.11	12,000
1.6.11 – 31.5.12	21,000

Using the pro forma layout provided, show the taxable profits for each tax year from 2010/11 to 2012/13.

Tax year	*Basis period*	*Taxable profits* £

THE CESSATION OF TRADING

You have seen the special basis period rules that apply in the first three years of a business. There are also special rules that apply in the last tax year that a business is carried on.

The final year of assessment is the tax year that the date of cessation falls into. The basis period for this final year normally runs from the end of the basis period for the previous year to the date of cessation.

Exceptionally, if a trade starts and ceases in the same tax year, the basis period for that year is the whole lifespan of the trade. If the final year is the second year, the basis period runs from 6 April at the start of the second year to the date of cessation.

Task 3

Malcolm has been trading for many years. His results for the last four periods of account before he ceased trading on 31 January 2012 are:

y/e 30.6.09	£12,000
y/e 30.6.10	£8,000
y/e 30.6.11	£6,000
p/e 31.01.12	£5,000

Using the pro forma layout provided show the taxable profits for the years 2009/10 to 2011/12 inclusive before considering any overlap relief (see below).

Tax year	*Basis period*	*Taxable profits* £
2009/10	1.7.08 - 30.6.09	12.000
2010/11	1.7.09 - 30.6.10	8.000
2011/12	1.7.10 - 31.1.12	11.000

OVERLAP PROFITS

You may have noticed above that the basis periods in the first three tax years of a new business may overlap with each other. This results in profits in the early years of a trade being taxed more than once.

Profits which have been taxed more than once are called OVERLAP PROFITS.

Some profits may be taxed twice because the basis period for the second tax year includes some or all of the period of trading in the first tax year or because the basis period for the third tax year overlaps with that for the second tax year.

HOW IT WORKS

Canning started a trade on 1 January 2010 and has the following results:

	£
1.1.10 – 30.6.10	28,500
1.7.10 – 30.6.11	48,000
1.7.11 – 30.6.12	70,000

The taxable profits are as follows.

Year	*Basis period*	*Working*	*Taxable profits*
			£
2009/10	1.1.10 – 5.4.10	£28,500 × 3/6	14,250
2010/11	1.1.10 – 31.12.10	£28,500 + £48,000 × 6/12	52,500
2011/12	1.7.10 – 30.6.11		48,000
2012/13	1.7.11 – 30.6.12		70,000

Overlap profits are:

	£
1.1.10 – 5.4.10	14,250
1.7.10 – 31.12.10	24,000
	38,250

Task 4

Harriet starts a trade on 1 March 2010, and has the following results.

Period	*Profit*
	£
1.3.10 – 30.6.11	32,000
1.7.11 – 30.6.12	36,800

(1) Using the pro forma layout provided, show the taxable profits for the first four tax years

Tax year	*Basis period*	*Taxable profits* £
2009/10	1.3.10 – 5.4.10	2000
2010/11	6.4.10 – 5.4.11	24000
2011/12	1.7.10 – 30.6.11	24000
2012/13	1.7.11 – 30.6.12	36800

(2) The overlap profits are:

£	18,000

When the trade ceases overlap profits are deducted from the final year's taxable profits. This means that over the life of a business, all of its total taxable profits, and no more, will have been taxed.

Task 5

Rex trades from 1 May 2007 to 31 January 2012, with the following results.

Period	*Profit*
	£
1.5.07 – 30.4.08	15,000
1.5.08 – 30.4.09	9,000
1.5.09 – 30.4.10	10,500
1.5.10 – 30.4.11	16,000
1.5.11 – 31.1.12	950
	51,450

Using the pro forma layout provided show the taxable profits for all relevant tax years.

Tax year	*Basis period*	*Taxable profits* £
Total taxable trading profits		

SELF EMPLOYMENT TAX RETURN PAGES

A copy of the page you will have to complete is available at the end of this chapter. You will be able to practise completing this form in the Business Tax Question Bank.

CHAPTER OVERVIEW

- The profits of a period of account ending in a tax year are normally taxed in that year
- In the first tax year, the basis period is the date the business starts to the following 5 April
- There are three possibilities in the second tax year:
  - If a period of account of 12 months or more ends in the second tax year, the basis period for the second tax year is the 12 months to the end of that period of account
  - If a period of account of less than 12 months ends in the second tax year, the basis period for the second tax year is the first 12 months from the start of trading
  - If no period of account ends in the second year, the basis period for that year is 6 April to 5 April in the year
- The basis period for the third tax year is the 12 months to the end of the period of account ending in that year
- The basis period in the final year of a business runs from the end of the previous basis period to the date that the trade stops
- When a trade ceases overlap profits are deducted from the final year's taxable profits

Keywords

Basis period – is the period whose profits are taxed in a tax year

Overlap profits – are the profits that are taxed more than once when a business starts

The tax year, **fiscal year** or **year of assessment** – is the year from 6 April in one year to 5 April in the next year

The current year basis of assessment – taxes the 12 month period of account ending in that tax year

TEST YOUR LEARNING

Test 1

Oliver starts to trade on 1 May 2011. He makes his first set of accounts up to 31 December 2011 and annually thereafter.

Fill in the following table setting out the basis periods for the first three tax years and the overlap period of profits.

Tax year	*Basis period*
Overlap profits	

Test 2

True or false: when the trade ceases overlap profits are deducted from the final year's taxable profits.

Test 3

Barlow stops trading on 31 December 2011 having been in business since January 2004. Previously he has always made accounts up to 31 May. Overlap profits on commencement were £10,000.

Results for the last few years (as adjusted for tax) are:

	Profits
	£
Period to 31.12.11	15,000
Year ended 31.5.11	25,000
Year ended 31.5.10	32,000
Year ended 31.5.09	18,000

Using the pro forma layout provided, compute the taxable profits for the final three years of trading.

Tax year	*Basis period*	*Taxable profits* £

Test 4

Amarjat started trading on 1 February 2011. He prepared his first accounts to 30 June 2012. Taxable profits for this 17 month period were £34,000. Show the taxable profits for 2010/11, 2011/12 and 2012/13. His overlap profits are:

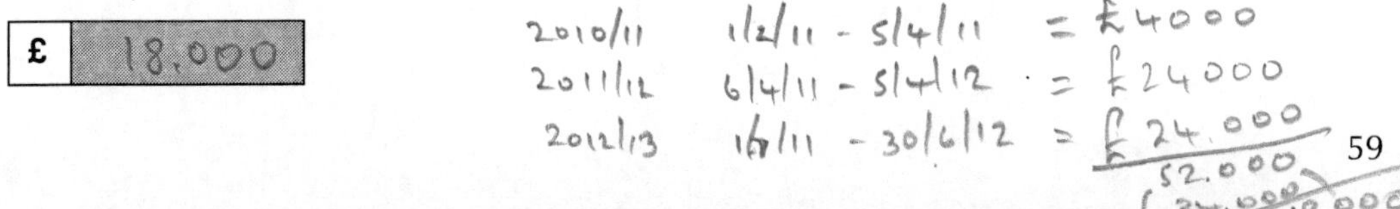

£	

Test 5

Susi started to trade on 1 December 2010. Her first accounts were prepared to 30 June 2011. Taxable profits for the first two periods of account were:

Period to 30 June 2011 £70,000

Year to 30 June 2012 £60,000

(1) Her taxable profits for 2010/11 are:

£	40,000

(2) Her taxable profits for 2011/12 are:

£	95,000

(3) Her taxable profits for 2012/13 are:

£	60,000

(4) Her overlap profits are:

£	65,000

2010/11 1/12/10 - 5/4/11 = £40,000

2011/12 1/12/10 - 30/11/11 = £95,000

2012/13 1/7/11 - 30/6/12 = £60,000

195,000

(130,000)

65,000

EXTRACT FROM SELF-EMPLOYMENT TAX RETURN

Business expenses

Read pages SEFN 7 to SEFN 9 of the *notes* to see what expenses are allowable for tax purposes.

Total expenses If your annual turnover was below £73,000 you may just put your total expenses in box 30		Disallowable expenses Use this column if the figures in boxes 16 to 29 include disallowable amounts	
16	Cost of goods bought for resale or goods used £ .00	31	£ .00
17	Construction industry - *payments to subcontractors* £ .00	32	£ .00
18	Wages, salaries and other staff costs £ .00	33	£ .00
19	Car, van and travel expenses £ .00	34	£ .00
20	Rent, rates, power and insurance costs £ .00	35	£ .00
21	Repairs and renewals of property and equipment £ .00	36	£ .00
22	Phone, fax, stationery and other office costs £ .00	37	£ .00
23	Advertising and business entertainment costs £ .00	38	£ .00
24	Interest on bank and other loans £ .00	39	£ .00
25	Bank, credit card and other financial charges £ .00	40	£ .00
26	Irrecoverable debts written off £ .00	41	£ .00
27	Accountancy, legal and other professional fees £ .00	42	£ .00
28	Depreciation and loss/profit on sale of assets £ .00	43	£ .00
29	Other business expenses £ .00	44	£ .00
30	Total expenses in boxes 16 to 29 £ .00	45	Total disallowable expenses in boxes 31 to 44 £ .00

SA103F 2011/12 Tax return: Self-employment (full): Page SEF 2 HMRC 12/09

chapter 5: PARTNERSHIPS

chapter coverage 🕮

You should recall that a partnership is a group of self employed individuals (partners) trading together. In this Chapter we will see how to compute a partnership's taxable trading profits and how these profits are divided between and taxed on the individual partners. We will look at situations where there is a change in the partnership profit sharing arrangements and where partners join or leave partnerships.

You may be asked to complete the tax return for a partnership.

The topics that we shall cover are:

- Computing taxable trading profits of partnerships
- Dividing taxable trading profits between partners
- The tax positions of individual partners
- Partnership investment income
- Partnership tax return

COMPUTING TAXABLE TRADING PROFITS OF PARTNERSHIPS

A partnership is a group of self employed individuals who are trading together.

A partnership prepares a trading income statement in exactly the same way as a sole trader would. This income statement is the income statement for the partnership business as a whole.

The net profit in the partnership income statement must be adjusted for tax purposes in exactly the same way as you would adjust the net profit in the accounts of a sole trader. This means that you must add back disallowable items. You must deduct specifically deductible items that have not been deducted in the accounts (for example capital allowances) and also any income in the accounts that is not part of the taxable trading profit. Finally, add any amounts taxable as trading profits that have not been included in the accounts. For example, the market value of any goods taken for own use.

A particular point worth noting is that any partners' salaries or interest on capital deducted in the accounts must be added back when computing taxable trading profits. These items are disallowable expenses because they are a form of drawings. They will be part of each partner's taxable trading profit as described below.

DIVIDING TAXABLE TRADING PROFITS BETWEEN PARTNERS

Once you have computed a partnership's taxable trading profit for a period of account you must divide it between the partners concerned.

The partners may agree to share profits in any way they wish. The agreed division will be set out in the partnership agreement and will always be stated for you in assessment tasks.

HOW IT WORKS

The Yellow partnership has tax adjusted profits of £40,000 for the year to 31 March 2012. The partners, Mr Blue and Mr Red have agreed to share profits three quarters to Mr Blue and one quarter to Mr Red.

For the year to 31 March 2012 , Mr Blue has taxable trading profits of £40,000 x ¾ = £30,000 and Mr Red has taxable trading profits of £40,000 x ¼ = £10,000.

Sometimes, rather than just divide profits between the partners in accordance with an agreed profit sharing ratio the partners may agree that some or all of the partners should:

(a) be paid a 'salary' and/or

(b) be paid interest on the capital they contributed to the partnership

In this case, your starting point in dividing a partnership's taxable profits between the partners should be to deal with any salary or interest on capital. Once you have done this you can divide the balance of any taxable trading profit between the partners in accordance with the profit sharing ratio.

HOW IT WORKS

Pearl and Ruby are in partnership. The partnership's taxable trading profits for the year ended 31 March 2012 were £110,000. The partnership agreement provides for Pearl to be paid a salary of £20,000 per annum and for Ruby to be paid a salary of £30,000 per annum. Any remaining profits are divided between Pearl and Ruby in the ratio 2:1.

First allocate the partners' salaries and then divide the balance of the profit in accordance with the profit sharing ratio:

	Total	**Pearl**	**Ruby**
	£	£	£
Salary	50,000	20,000	30,000
Profit (£110,000 – £30,000 – £20,000)	60,000	40,000	20,000
	110,000	60,000	50,000

Pearl has taxable profits of £60,000 and Ruby has taxable profits of £50,000 for the year ended 31 March 2012.

Task 1

Roger and Muggles are in partnership. Tax adjusted trading profits for the year to 31 December 2011 were £210,000. The partnership agreement states that profits should be divided between Roger and Muggles in the ratio 4:1 after paying a salary of £30,000 per annum to each of the partners.

The taxable trading profit for Roger for the year to 31 December 2011 is:

and the taxable trading profit for Muggles for the year to 31 December 2011 is:

You should approach questions where the partnership agreement provides for interest on capital in exactly the same way. This means that you should allocate any interest on capital to the partners before dividing the balance of the profit in the agreed profit sharing ratio.

HOW IT WORKS

Sunita and Jim have been trading in partnership for several years. The partnership prepares accounts to 31 December each year and the taxable trading profits for the year to 31 December 2011 are £140,000. The partnership agreement provides for the following salaries, rates of interest on capital and share of remaining profits:

	Salary per annum	*Interest on capital*	*Division of profit*
	£	%	%
Sunita	45,000	3	50
Jim	25,000	3	50

The capital account balances of Sunita and Jim are £40,000 and £10,000 respectively.

The profits of the year to 31 December 2011 are allocated between the partners in the following way:

	Total	*Sunita*	*Jim*
	£	£	£
Salary	70,000	45,000	25,000
Interest on capital (3%)	1,500	1,200	300
Profits (£140,000 – 70,000 – 1,500)	68,500	34,250	34,250
Taxable profits	140,000	80,450	59,550

Task 2

James, Kieran and Jemima are in partnership. For the year to 31 December 2011 taxable trading profits were £270,000. They contributed capital of £20,000 each to the partnership. The partnership agreement provides for interest on capital of 5% to each party and salaries of £35,000 to be paid to Kieran and Jemima. James is not paid a salary. Remaining profits are divided between James, Kieran and Jemima in the ratio 3:1:1.

Using the pro forma layout provided, show how these profits for the year to 31 December 2011 are allocated between the partners.

	Total	James	Kieran	Jemima
	£	£	£	£
SALARY	70,000	0	35000	35,000
INTEREST	3000	1000	1000	1000
PROFITS	197,000	118200	39400	39400
TAXABLE	270,000	119200	75400	75400

Change in the profit sharing agreement

Sometimes the agreed profit sharing arrangements may change during a period of account. If this happens you should time apportion the profits to before and after the change and then divide them between the partners.

HOW IT WORKS

Jenny and Chris are in partnership. Taxable trading profits of the partnership for the year ended 31 March 2012 are £60,000. Until 30 September 2011 profits are shared equally. From 1 October 2011 Jenny and Chris agree that the profits should be shared in the ratio 2:1.

Show how the taxable trading profits of the year to 31 March 2012 are divided between Jenny and Chris.

Your first step should be to apportion the profits to the periods before and after the change in the profit sharing ratio:

1.4.11 – 30.9.11 6/12 × £60,000 = £30,000

1.10.11 – 31.3.12 6/12 × £60,000 = £30,000

Next divide these profits between the partners:

	Total	***Jenny***	***Chris***
	£	£	£
1.4.11 – 30.9.11	30,000	15,000	15,000
1.10.11 – 31.3.12	30,000	20,000	10,000
	60,000	35,000	25,000

For the year to 31 March 2012, Jenny's taxable trading profits are £35,000 and Chris' taxable trading profits are £25,000.

Task 3

Hansel and Greta are in partnership. The partnership accounts are prepared to 30 June each year. The taxable trading profits for the year ended 30 June 2011 were £80,000. Until 31 March 2011 Hansel and Greta shared profits equally. From 1 April 2011 they shared profits in the ratio 4:1.

(1) Using the pro forma layout provided, show how the profits are apportioned between the periods before and after the change in profit sharing ratio:

	£
1/7/10 – 31/3/11 £80,000 x 9/12	60,000
1/4/11 – 30/6/11 £80,000 x 3/12	20,000
TAXABLE PROFITS	80,000

(2) Using the pro forma layout provided, calculate the taxable profits for each partner for the year to 30 June 2011.

	Total	*Hansel*	*Greta*
	£	£	£
1/7/10 – 31/3/11	60,000	30,000	30,000
1/4/11 – 30/6/11	20,000	16,000	4000
TAXABLE PROFIT	80,000	46,000	34,000

A change in the rate at which salaries or interest are paid during a period of account has similar implications. You should time apportion the profits before and after the change and deal with each period separately. Remember that the salaries and interest will need to be time apportioned too.

THE TAX POSITIONS OF INDIVIDUAL PARTNERS

Once you have allocated taxable profits for a period of account between partners you must decide which tax year the profits are taxed in.

The current year basis of assessment applies to partnerships in the same way as it does to sole traders. For example, if a partnership prepares accounts to 30 June each year, the year to 30 June 2011 is the basis period for 2011/12 and a partner will be taxed on his share of the profits arising in the year ended 30 June 2011 in 2011/12.

Changes in partners

Sometimes the partners within a partnership change. If a new partner joins a partnership, the special opening year rules that we saw earlier in this Text for sole traders apply to the new partner. The existing partners continue to be taxed using the current year basis of assessment.

Similarly, if a partner leaves a partnership the closing year rules apply to that partner as though he were a sole trader but the other partners continue to be taxed using the current year basis of assessment.

HOW IT WORKS: PARTNER JOINING A PARTNERSHIP

Francis and Caroline have been in partnership for many years making up accounts to 31 December each year. Profits were shared equally until 1 June 2010, when Charles joined the partnership. From 1 June 2010 profits were shared in the ratio 2:2:1.

Profits adjusted for tax purposes are as follows.

Period	***Taxable profit***
	£
1.1.10 – 31.12.10	48,000
1.1.11 – 31.12.11	18,000
1.1.12 – 31.12.12	24,000

Show the taxable profits for each partner for 2010/11 to 2012/13.

We must first share the profits between the partners.

	Total	***Francis***	***Caroline***	***Charles***
	£	£	£	£
Year ended 31.12.10				
1.1.10 – 31.5.10 (5/12)				
Profits 50:50	20,000	10,000	10,000	
1.6.10 – 31.12.10 (7/12)				
Profits 2:2:1	28,000	11,200	11,200	5,600
Total	48,000	21,200	21,200	5,600
Year ended 31.12.11				
Profits	18,000	7,200	7,200	3,600
Total for y/e 31.12.11	18,000	7,200	7,200	3,600
Year ended 31.12.12				
Profits	24,000	9,600	9,600	4,800
Total for y/e 31.12.12	24,000	9,600	9,600	4,800

The next stage is to work out the basis periods and hence the taxable profits for the partners in each tax year. The most important thing to remember at this stage is to deal with each of the partners separately.

Francis and Caroline are taxed on the current year basis of assessment throughout.

Year	*Basis period*	*Francis*	*Caroline*
		£	£
2010/11	1.1.10 – 31.12.10	21,200	21,200
2011/12	1.1.11– 31.12.11	7,200	7,200
2012/13	1.1.12 – 31.12.12	9,600	9,600

Charles joins the partnership on 1 June 2010 with falls in tax year 2010/11 so the opening year rules apply to him from 2010/11.

Year	*Basis period*	*Working*	*Taxable profits*
			£
2010/11	1.6.10 – 5.4.11	£5,600 + 3/12 × £3,600	6,500
2011/12	1.1.11 – 31.12.11		3,600
2012/13	1.1.12 – 31.12.12		4,800

Charles has overlap profits of £900 to carry forward and relieve in the tax year in which he leaves the partnership.

HOW IT WORKS: PARTNER LEAVING A PARTNERSHIP

Dominic, Sebastian and India have traded in partnership sharing profits equally for many years. On 1 May 2011 India left the partnership. Profits continue to be shared equally. Accounts have always been prepared to 30 September and recent results have been:

	Profit
	£
Y/e 30.9.09	36,000
Y/e 30.9.10	81,000
Y/e 30.9.11	60,000

Each of the partners had overlap profits of £10,000 on commencement of the business. Show the taxable trading profits of each partner for 2009/10 to 2011/12.

Firstly allocate the profits of each period of account to the partners.

	Total	*Dominic*	*Sebastian*	*India*
	£	£	£	£
Y/e 30.9.09	36,000	12,000	12,000	12,000
Y/e 30.9.10	81,000	27,000	27,000	27,000
Y/e 30.9.11				
1.10.10 – 30.4.11 (7/12)	35,000	11,667	11,667	11,666
1.5.11 – 30.9.11 (5/12)	25,000	12,500	12,500	–
	60,000	24,167	24,167	11,666

Dominic and Sebastian are taxed on the continuing basis of assessment throughout:

	Dominic	**Sebastian**
	£	£
2009/10 (y/e 30.9.09)	12,000	12,000
2010/11 (y/e 30.9.10)	27,000	27,000
2011/12 (y/e 30.9.11)	24,167	24,167

India is treated as ceasing to trade in 2011/12.

	£
2009/10 (y/e 30.9.09)	12,000
2010/11 (y/e 30.9.10)	27,000
2011/12 (p/e 30.4.11 – overlap profits) (£11,666 – £10,000)	1,666

Task 4

A partnership makes profits as follows.

	£
Year ended 31 October 2010	34,200
Year ended 31 October 2011	45,600

A partner joins on 1 June 2010 and is entitled to 30% of the profits.

His taxable profits for 2010/11 are:

£	

His overlap profits carried forward are:

£	

His taxable profits for 2011/12 are:

£	

Task 5

X, Y and Z have traded in partnership for many years sharing profits equally. On 1 July 2010 X retired. Y and Z continue trading, sharing profits in the ratio 3:2.

There were no unrelieved overlap profits on commencement of the business.

The profits of the partnership as adjusted for tax purposes are as follows.

	Profit
	£
Year to 31 March 2010	24,000
Year to 31 March 2011	14,000
Year to 31 March 2012	48,000

(1) Using the pro forma layout provided, show the division of partnership profits in the three years to 31 March 2012:

	Total	*X*	*Y*	*Z*
	£	£	£	£
YR TO 31 MARCH 2010	24,000	8000	8000	8000
1.4.10 – 1.7.10	3,500	1167	1167	1166
1.7.10 – 31.3.11	10,500	0	6300	4200
1.4.10 – 31.3.12	48,000	0	28800	19,200

(2) Using the information from part (1) complete the following table showing the amounts taxable on each partner in the relevant tax years:

	X	Y	Z
2009/10	8000	8000	8000
2010/11	1167	7467	5366
2011/12	0	28800	19,200

PARTNERSHIP INVESTMENT INCOME

A partnership may also have investment income such as interest on a bank account.

Partnership investment income is shared between partners in a similar way to trading income using the profit sharing ratios applicable to the period in which the investment income accrues.

PARTNERSHIP TAX RETURN

In your assessment you may be asked to complete the partnership summary of the partnership tax return. A copy of this page is available at the end of this chapter. You will be able to practise completing this return in the Business Tax Question Bank.

CHAPTER OVERVIEW

- A partnership is a group of self employed individuals trading together
- Calculate tax adjusted profits for a partnership in the same way as you would calculate the tax adjusted profits of a sole trader
- Divide the tax adjusted profits of a period of account between the partners in accordance with their profit sharing arrangements during the period of account
- If profit sharing arrangements change during a period of account, time apportion profits to the periods before and after the change before allocating them to partners
- Once you have found a partner's profit for a period of account you can consider which tax year that profit is taxed in. A continuing partner in a continuing business is taxed using the current year basis of assessment
- The opening year rules apply to a partner joining the partnership. The closing year rules apply to a partner leaving the partnership

TEST YOUR LEARNING

Test 1

The adjusted profit of a partnership is divided between the partners in accordance with the profit sharing agreement in existence during what period?

A the calendar year
B the tax year
C the period of account concerned
D the period agreed by the partners

Test 2

Dave and Joe are in partnership together and make a profit of £18,000 for the year to 31 December 2011. Up to 30 September 2011 they share profits and losses equally but thereafter they share 3:2.

18.000 × 9/12 = 13,500
18.000 × 3/12 = 4500

Dave's taxable profits for 2011/12 are:

£	9450

and Joe's taxable profits for 2011/12 are:

£	8550

DAVE	JOE
6750	6750
2700	1800
9450	8550

Test 3

Sunita and Jasmine are in partnership sharing profits equally after paying a salary of £5,000 to Sunita and a salary of £80,000 to Jasmine. Taxable profits for the year to 31 March 2012 were £200,000.

Using the pro forma layout provided, show the taxable profits of each of the partners for the year.

	Total	***Sunita***	***Jasmine***
	£	**£**	**£**
SALARY	85000	5000	80000
PROFITS	115.000	57500	57500
TAXABLE PROFITS	200,000	62,500	137.500

Test 4

Barry and Steve have been in partnership for many years. Profits are shared three-quarters to Barry and one-quarter to Steve. For the year ended 31 March 2011, the partnership made a profit of £60,000 and for the year ended 31 March 2012 the profit was £80,000.

The profit taxable on Steve for 2011/12 is:

A £60,000
B £15,000
C £45,000
D £20,000

Test 5

Abdul and Ghita have been in partnership for many years. On 1 September 2011, Sase joins the partnership and profits are shared 2:2:1. For the year to 31 August 2012, the partnership makes a profit of £120,000.

The profits assessable on Sase in 2011/12 are:

The profits assessable on Sase in 2012/13 are:

The overlap profits arising for Sase are:

£

Test 6

William, Ann and John have been in partnership for many years sharing profits equally. Accounts have always been prepared to 31 October each year. All partners had overlap profits of £5,000 on commencement. On 31 December 2011 William left the partnership. Profits continued to be shared equally. Recent results were:

	£
Y/e 31 October 2010	21,000
Y/e 31 October 2011	33,000
Y/e 31 October 2012	36,000

(1) Using the pro forma layout provided, show how the profits of each period will be divided between the partners.

	Total	William	Ann	John
	£	£	£	£
Y/E 31/10/10	21,000	7000	7000	7000
Y/E 31/10/11	33,000	11000	11000	11000
Y/E 31/10/12				
1.11.11 - 31.12.11	6000	2000	2000	2000
1.1.12 - 31.10.12	30000	0	15,000	15000

(2) Using the pro forma layout provided, show the taxable profits for each partner for 2010/11 to 2012/13.

	Ann	John	William
	£	£	£
2010/11	7000	7000	7000
2011/12	11000	11000	3000
2012/13	17000	17,000	0

EXTRACT FROM PARTNERSHIP TAX RETURN

PARTNERSHIP STATEMENT (SHORT) *for tax return to year end 5 April 2012*

Please read these instructions before completing the Statement

Use these pages to allocate partnership income if the only income for the relevant return period was trading and professional income or taxed interest and alternative finance receipts from banks and building societies. Otherwise you must ask the SA Orderline for the *Partnership Statement (Full)* pages to record details of the allocation of all the partnership income.

Step 1 Fill in boxes 1 to 29 and boxes A and B as appropriate. Get the figures you need from the relevant boxes in the Partnership Tax Return. Complete a separate Statement for each accounting period covered by this Partnership Tax Return and for each trade or profession carried on by the partnership.

Step 2 Then allocate the amounts in boxes 11 to 29 attributable to each partner using the allocation columns on this page and page 7 (see pages 14 to 17 of the Partnership Tax Return Guide for help). If the partnership has more than three partners, please photocopy page 7.

Step 3 Each partner will need a copy of their allocation of income to fill in their personal tax return.

PARTNERSHIP INFORMATION

If the partnership business includes a trade or profession, enter here the accounting period for which appropriate items in this statement are returned.

Start **1** / /

End **2** / /

Nature of trade **3**

MIXED PARTNERSHIPS

Tick here if this Statement is drawn up using Corporation Tax rules **4**

Tick here if this Statement is drawn up using tax rules for non-residents **5**

Individual partner details

6 Name of partner

Address

Postcode

Date appointed as a partner (if during 2010–11 or 2011–12) **7** / /

Partner's unique taxpayer reference (UTR) **8**

Date ceased to be a partner (if during 2010–11 or 2011–12) **9** / /

Partner's National Insurance number **10**

Partnership's profits, losses, income, tax credits, etc.	Tick this box if the items entered in the box had foreign tax taken off		Partner's share of profits, losses, income, tax credits, etc.	Copy figures in boxes 11 to 29 to boxes in the individual's Partnership (short) pages as shown below
• for an accounting period ended in 2011–12	▼			
from box 3.83 Profit from a trade or profession	A	11 £	Profit 11 £	Copy this figure to box 7
from box 3.82 Adjustment on change of basis		11A £	11A £	Copy this figure to box 9
from box 3.84 Loss from a trade or profession	B	12 £	Loss 12 £	Copy this figure to box 7
• for the period 6 April 2011 to 5 April 2012*				
from box 7.9A UK taxed interest and taxed alternative finance receipts		22 £	22 £	Copy this figure to box 26
from box 3.97 CIS deductions made by contractors on account of tax		24 £	24 £	Copy this figure to box 28
from box 3.98 Other tax taken off trading income		24A £	24A £	Copy this figure to box 29
from box 7.8A Income Tax taken off		25 £	25 £	Copy this figure to box 27
from box 3.117 Partnership charges		29 £	29 £	Copy this figure to box 4, 'Other tax reliefs' section on page Ai 2 in your personal tax return

* If you are a 'CT Partnership' see page 4 of the Partnership Tax Return Guide

HMRC 12/09 PARTNERSHIP TAX RETURN: PAGE 6

chapter 6:
LOSSES

chapter coverage

So far in this Text we have seen how to compute taxable trading profits. Sometimes the result of this computation is a loss rather than a profit. In this chapter we will cover the various methods by which a taxpayer may obtain relief for such a loss.

The topic that we shall cover is:

- Losses in a continuing business

LOSSES IN A CONTINUING BUSINESS

As you know, the starting point for computing a business' trading results is to take the income statement and adjust it for tax purposes. If this adjusted figure is negative then there is a trading loss rather than a taxable profit. This has two implications:

(a) The loss is a loss of the tax year for which the period of account concerned formed the basis period. However, the amount taxable in that tax year is Nil. It is not the negative amount.

(b) The amount of the trading loss is equal to the tax adjusted negative figure. The taxpayer has a choice as to how this is relieved as explained below.

HOW IT WORKS

If a trader makes a loss of £5,000 in the year to 31 December 2011, the 2011/12 taxable profits based on that period will be £nil. There will be a trading loss in 2011/12 of £5,000. The taxpayer can choose to relieve the 2011/12 loss in the ways discussed below.

The alternative ways in which a trading loss can be relieved are as follows:

(a) The loss can be carried forward and deducted from taxable trading profits arising from the same trade in future years. If this option is chosen the loss must be used as quickly as possible. If the following year's taxable profits are less than the amount of the loss, then those profits will be reduced to Nil and the balance of the loss carried forward to relieve in future years. The loss can be carried forward indefinitely until it is relieved.

(b) The loss can be deducted from total income in the tax year of the loss. You should recall from Chapter 1 that total income is the total of a taxpayer's income from all sources. Consequently total income may include rental income, employment income, interest and dividends.

(c) Whether or not option (b) is chosen, the loss can be deducted from total income in the tax year preceding the tax year of the loss.

A taxpayer does not have to deduct a loss under either (b) or (c) above if he does not wish to do so. If he does wish to make either of these deductions he must make a claim to do so. Claims to deduct a loss must be made by the 31 January that is 22 months after the end of the tax year of the loss ie by 31 January 2014 for a loss in 2011/12.

If a taxpayer has sufficient loss to deduct under both (b) and (c) he can choose to make one or both of the deductions. He can also choose the order of the deductions. However, once a claim is made all of the available loss must be deducted. Partial claims are not possible.

Any loss remaining after any claims under (b) and (c) above have been made, is automatically carried forward to deduct under (a) against the first available trading profits.

HOW IT WORKS

Ahmed, a sole trader, has the following taxable trading profits/(loss):

	£
Year to 30 September 2010 (and so taxed in 2010/11)	10,000
Year to 30 September 2011 (loss, no trading profits to tax in 2011/12)	(59,000)
Year to 30 September 2012 (and so taxed in 2012/13)	20,000

His only other income is rental income of £15,000 a year.

The loss of £59,000 is a loss of 2011/12. This loss could be deducted from total income of £25,000 (trading income of £10,000 + rental income of £15,000) in 2010/11 and/or from total income (rental income) of £15,000 in 2011/12. If both of these claims are made, the loss not relieved of £19,000 is automatically deducted from the taxable trading profits of £20,000 arising in 2012/13.

Ahmed does not have to claim to deduct the loss from total income in 2010/11 and/or 2011/12. If he does not make a claim to deduct the loss from total income, the loss is carried forward to deduct from taxable trading profits in future years.

The disadvantage of deducting a loss from total income in the year of the loss and/or in the preceding year is that personal allowances may be wasted. You will recall that every individual has a personal allowance that he can set against his net income. Income of up to the personal allowance is effectively tax free income so there is no benefit if the net income is reduced to an amount less than the personal allowance.

HOW IT WORKS

Sase has a loss in her period of account ending 31 December 2011 of £13,000. In the year to 31 December 2010 she made a profit of £5,000. Her other income is £9,000 a year and she wishes to claim loss relief for the year of loss and then for the preceding year.

Assuming that the personal allowance was £7,475 in both 2010/11 and 2011/12, Sase's taxable income for each year is calculated in the following way.

The loss-making period ends in 2011/12, so the year of the loss is 2011/12. The trading profit of £5,000 for the year to 31 December 2010 is taxed in 2010/11.

	2010/11	***2011/12***
	£	£
Total income	14,000	9,000
Less loss relief	(4,000)	(9,000)
Net income	10,000	NIL

You can see that in 2011/12, Sase's personal allowance will be wasted. If Sase claims loss relief in the year there is nothing she can do about this waste of relief. Alternatively, Sase could make the 2010/11 claim and not the 2011/12 claim. This would leave net income of £1,000 in 2010/11 to set the personal allowance against, with the remainder of the personal allowance in 2010/11 wasted.

Task

In 2011/12 Niahla makes a loss of £30,000. Her total income in 2011/12 is £21,000, and her personal allowance for that year is £7,475. She has no other source of income for any other year. If she obtains loss relief as soon as possible, the loss carried forward for future relief is:

£	

CHAPTER OVERVIEW

- A trading loss can be

  (a) carried forward to be deducted from the first available profits of the same trade

  (b) deducted from total income in the tax year of the loss and/or in the preceding tax year

Any loss not deducted under (b) above is automatically carried forward for deduction under (a)

TEST YOUR LEARNING

Test 1

Harold, who has been in business for many years, makes a trading loss of £20,000 in the year ended 31 January 2012. In which year(s) may the loss be relieved, assuming relief is claimed as soon as possible?

A 2011/12 only
B 2012/13 and/or 2011/12
C 2010/11 only
D 2011/12 and/or 2010/11

Test 2

True/false: trading losses can only be carried forward for deduction in the six succeeding tax years.

Test 3

Where losses are carried forward, against what sort of income may they be relieved?

A Against non-savings income
B Against total income
C Against trading income arising in the same trade
D Against trading income arising in all trades carried on by the taxpayer

Test 4

Mallory, who has traded for many years, has the following tax adjusted results:

Year ended 30 April 2010	Profit	£10,000
Year ended 30 April 2011	Loss	£(40,000)
Year ended 30 April 2012	Profit	£25,000

Mallory has other income of £9,000 each year. Explain how the loss in the year to 30 April 2011 can be relieved.

chapter 7: NATIONAL INSURANCE

chapter coverage 📖

In this chapter we see that the self employed must pay two types of national insurance contribution (NIC). We will see how to calculate these contributions.

The topic that we shall cover is:

✍ NICs payable by the self employed

NICS PAYABLE BY THE SELF EMPLOYED

The self employed (ie sole traders and partners) must pay two types of NIC:

(a) CLASS 2 CONTRIBUTIONS, and
(b) CLASS 4 CONTRIBUTIONS

Class 2 contributions are payable at a flat rate of £2.50 a week. It is possible to be excepted from Class 2 contributions if annual profits are less than £5,315. An individual who starts to trade must notify HMRC that he is liable to Class 2 contributions. There is a penalty for failure to notify if notification is not made before 31 January following the end of the tax year in which trade started.

Class 4 contributions are based on the level of the individual's trading profits. Main rate contributions are calculated by applying a fixed percentage (9% for 2011/12) to the individual's profits between the annual lower profits limit (LPL) (£7,225 for 2011/12) and the annual upper profits limit (UPL) (£42,475 for 2011/12). Additional rate contributions are 2% on profits above the annual upper profits limit.

The rates of Class 2 and Class 4 NICs will be given to you in the assessment.

HOW IT WORKS

If Jon had taxable trading profits of £46,000 for 2011/12 his Class 4 liability would be calculated in the following way:

	£
Annual upper profits limit	42,475
Less: annual lower profits limit	(7,225)
	35,250

		£
Class 4 NICs =	9% × £35,250	3,172.50
	2% × (46,000 – 42,475)	70.50
Total		3,243.00

In addition Jon would pay Class 2 contributions of (52 × £2.50) = £130.00.

Task 1

Lawrence, who is a sole trader, had taxable profits of £25,000 for 2011/12. The NICs he must pay are:

Class 2

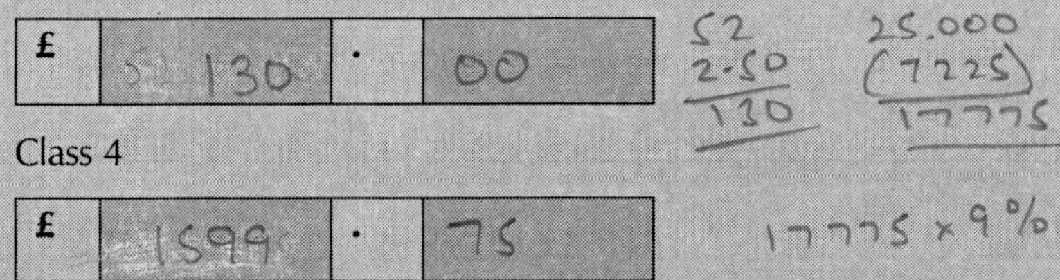

Class 4

Task 2

Amelia had taxable partnership profits of £60,000 for 2011/12.

Her total NICs payable for 2011/12 are:

60,000
(7225)
52,775

A £3,653.00
B £4,879.75
C £3,523.00
D £4,749.75

9% × 35.250 = 3172.50
2% × 17,525 = 350.50
52 × 2.50 = 130.00
3653.00

CHAPTER OVERVIEW

- Self employed traders pay

  (a) Class 2 contributions at a flat rate per week (£2.50 in 2011/12) and
  (b) Class 4 contributions based on the level of their profits

- Main rate Class 4 NICs are 9% of profits between the UPL and LPL
- Additional Class 4 NICs are 2% of profits above the UPL

Keywords

Class 2 contributions – are flat rate contributions payable by the self employed

Class 4 contributions – are profit related contributions payable by the self employed

TEST YOUR LEARNING

Compute the following sole traders' liabilities to NICs for 2011/12.

Test 1

Acker

Taxable trading profits £5,050

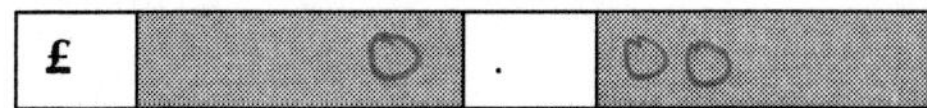

Test 2

Bailey

Taxable trading profits £50,000

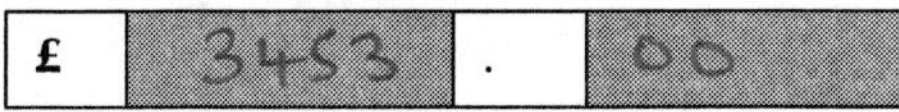

Text 3

Cartwright

Taxable trading profits £10,850

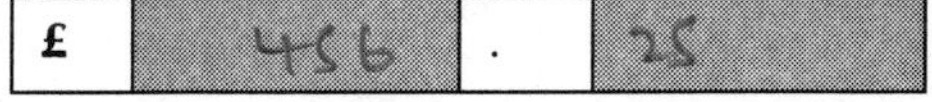

chapter 8: SELF ASSESSMENT FOR INDIVIDUALS

chapter coverage

In this chapter we look at when tax returns must be filed, for how long records must be kept and at the penalties chargeable for failure to comply with the requirements.

We then look at the due dates for payment of income tax and the consequences of late payment.

Finally, we consider the important topic of client confidentiality.

The topics covered are:

- Tax returns and keeping records
- Penalties
- Payment of tax, interest and penalties for late payment
- Enquiries

TAX RETURNS AND KEEPING RECORDS

An individual's tax return comprises a Tax Form, together with supplementary pages for particular sources of income and capital gains. We will look at self assessment of income tax in this Chapter. The self assessment of capital gains is very similar but we will consider it in detail later in this Text.

Notice of chargeability

Individuals who are chargeable to tax for any tax year and who have not received a notice to file a return are, in general, required to give notice of chargeability within six months from the end of the year, ie by 5 October 2012 for 2011/12.

Filing tax returns

The FILING DUE DATE is:

- For paper returns – 31 October following the end of the tax year that the return covers, eg for 2011/12 by 31 October 2012.
- For returns filed online – 31 January following the end of the tax year that the return covers, eg for 2011/12 by 31 January 2013.

Where a notice to make a return is issued after 31 October following the tax year a period of three months is allowed for the online filing of that return. Where a notice to make a return is issued after 31 July following the tax year a period of three months is allowed for the filing of a paper return.

An individual may ask HMRC to make the tax computation if a paper return is filed. Where an online return is filed, the tax computation is made automatically.

HOW IT WORKS

Advise the following clients of the latest filing date for their personal tax return for 2011/12 if the return is:

(a) Paper
(b) Online

Norma	Notice to file tax return issued by HMRC on 6 April 2012
Melanie	Notice to file tax return issued by HMRC on 10 August 2012
Olga	Notice to file tax return issued by HMRC on 12 December 2012

The latest filing dates are:

	Paper	**Online**
Norma	31 October 2012	31 January 2013
Melanie	9 November 2012	31 January 2013
Olga	11 March 2013	11 March 2013

Task 1

HMRC issued a notice to file a tax return for 2011/12 to Myer on 3 November 2012. She filed this return online on 31 March 2013. State the date by which the return should have been filed:

Keeping of records

Taxpayers must keep and retain all records required to enable them to make and deliver a correct tax return.

In general, records must be retained by tax payers until the later of:

(a) One year after the 31 January following the tax year concerned

(b) Five years after 31 January following the tax year concerned if the taxpayer is in business or has property business income

PENALTIES

Penalties for error

A penalty may be imposed where a taxpayer makes an inaccurate return if he has:

(a) Been careless because he has not taken reasonable care in making the return or discovers the error later but does not take reasonable steps to inform HMRC

(b) Made a deliberate error but does not make arrangements to conceal it

(c) Made a deliberate error and has attempted to conceal it, eg by submitting false evidence in support of an inaccurate figure

An error which is made where the taxpayer has taken reasonable care in making the return and which he does not discover later, does not result in a penalty.

In order for a penalty to be charged, the inaccurate return must result in:

(a) An understatement of the taxpayer's tax liability
(b) A false or increased loss for the taxpayer
(c) A false or increased repayment of tax to the taxpayer

If a return contains more than one error, a penalty can be charged for each error. The rules also extend to errors in claims for allowances and reliefs and in accounts submitted in relation to tax liability.

The amount of the penalty for error is based on the Potential Lost Revenue (PLR) to HMRC as a result of the error. For example, if there is an understatement of tax, this understatement will be the PLR.

The maximum amount of the penalty for error depends on the type of error.

Type of error	**Maximum penalty payable**
Careless	30% of PLR
Deliberate but not concealed	70% of PLR
Deliberate and concealed	100% of PLR

A penalty for error may be reduced if the taxpayer tells HMRC about the error – this is called a disclosure. The reduction depends on the circumstances of the disclosure and the help that the taxpayer gives to HMRC in relation to the disclosure.

An unprompted disclosure is one made at a time when the taxpayer has no reason to believe HMRC has discovered, or is about to discover, the error. Otherwise, the disclosure will be a prompted disclosure. The minimum penalties that can be imposed are as follows.

Type of error	Unprompted	Prompted
Careless	0% of PLR	15% of PLR
Deliberate but not concealed	20% of PLR	35% of PLR
Deliberate and concealed	30% of PLR	50% of PLR

You will see that an unprompted disclosure where a careless mistake has been made can reduce a penalty for error to nil and all penalties can be reduced by half if the taxpayer makes a prompted disclosure.

A penalty for a careless error may be suspended by HMRC to allow the taxpayer to take action to ensure that the error does not occur again (eg where the error has arisen from failure to keep proper records).

HMRC will impose conditions which the taxpayer has to satisfy, eg establishing proper recordkeeping systems.

The penalty will be cancelled if the conditions imposed by HMRC are complied with by the taxpayer within a period of up to two years.

A taxpayer can appeal against:

(a) The penalty being charged
(b) The amount of the penalty
(c) A decision by HMRC not to suspend a penalty
(d) The conditions set by HMRC in relation to the suspension of a penalty

Task 2

Kelly deliberately omitted an invoice from her trading income in her 2011/12 tax return, but did not destroy the evidence. She later disclosed this error, before she had reason to believe HMRC might investigate the matter.

Complete the following sentence:

Kelly's penalty can be reduced from ....% of the potential lost revenue (for a deliberate, but not concealed error) to ....%, with the unprompted disclosure of her error.

Penalties for late notification

A penalty can be charged for failure to notify chargeability to income tax and/or capital gains tax. Penalties are behaviour related, increasing for more serious failures, and are again based on 'potential lost revenue'.

The minimum and maximum penalties as percentages of PLR are as follows:

Behaviour	Maximum penalty	Minimum penalty with unprompted disclosure		Minimum penalty with prompted disclosure	
Deliberate and concealed	100%	30%		50%	
Deliberate but not concealed	70%	20%		35%	
		>12m	<12m	>12m	<12m
Careless	30%	10%	0%	20%	10%

There is no zero penalty for reasonable care (as there is for penalties for errors on returns – see above), although the penalty may be reduced to 0% if the failure is rectified within 12 months through unprompted disclosure. The penalties may also be reduced at HMRC's discretion in 'special circumstances'. Inability to pay the penalty is not a 'special circumstance'.

The same penalties apply for failure to notify HMRC of a new taxable activity.

Where the taxpayer's failure is not 'deliberate', there is no penalty if he can show he has a 'reasonable excuse'. Reasonable excuse does not include having insufficient money to pay the penalty. Taxpayers can appeal against penalty decisions.

Penalties for late filing

The maximum penalties for filing a late tax return are:

(a) Initial penalty for late filing of £100
(b) If the return is more than 3 months late a daily penalty of £10 may be payable for a period of up to 90 days
(c) If the return is more than 6 months but less than 12 months late the penalty is 5% of the tax due
(d) If the return is more than 12 months late the penalty is
  - 100% of the tax due where withholding of information is deliberate and concealed
  - 70% of the tax due where withholding of information is deliberate but not concealed
  - 5% of the tax due in other cases (eg careless)

These tax based penalties (c and d above) are all subject to a minimum of £300.

Penalties for failure to keep records

The maximum penalty for each failure to keep and retain records is £3,000 per tax year.

PAYMENT OF TAX, INTEREST AND PENALTIES FOR LATE PAYMENT

Payments of tax

A taxpayer must make three payments of income tax and Class 4 NICs:

Date	**Payment**
31 January in the tax year	First payment on account
31 July after the tax year	Second payment on account
31 January after the tax year	Final payment to settle any remaining liability

Each PAYMENT ON ACCOUNT is equal to 50% of the income tax payable (after the deduction of PAYE and tax suffered at source) plus Class 4 NICs for the previous year.

Class 2 NICs can be collected monthly or twice yearly by direct debit, or paid twice yearly in response to requests issued by HMRC. Monthly direct debits are collected four months in arrears, so payments for 2011/12 would start in August 2011. Half yearly payments are due by 31 Jan during the tax year and 31 July after the end of the tax year. So for 2011/12, the first six months worth of Class 2 NICs would be paid by 31 January 2012 and the second six months worth by 31 July 2012. Payment by direct debit, as opposed to in response to a request from HMRC, would therefore ensure these deadlines are met.

HOW IT WORKS

Jeremy had income tax payable for 2011/12 of £12,000.

Each payment on account for 2012/13 is £12,000/2 = £6,000.

Task 3

Karen's income tax payable and Class 4 NICs for 2011/12 totalled £14,000. She estimates that her income tax payable and Class 4 NICs for 2012/13 will be £16,000.

What payments on account must Karen make for 2012/13 and when are they due?

£7000/31 JAN 2013

£7000/31 JUL 2013

Payments on account are not required if the income tax payable for the previous year is less than £1,000, or if more than 80% of the previous year's liability was paid by tax deducted at source.

Payments on account are normally fixed by reference to the previous year's tax liability but if a taxpayer expects his liability to be lower than this he may claim to reduce his payments on account to:

(a) A stated amount
(b) Nil

If the taxpayer's eventual liability is higher than he estimated (after making such a claim) he will have reduced the payments on account too far. Although the payments on account will not be adjusted, the taxpayer will suffer an interest charge on late payment.

The balance of any income tax is normally payable on or before the 31 January following the year.

HOW IT WORKS

Jameel made payments on account for 2011/12 of £7,500 each on 31 January 2012 and 31 July 2012, based on his 2010/11 liability. He later calculates his total income tax payable for 2011/12 at £20,000.

The final payment for 2011/12 is £20,000 - £7,500 - £7,500 = £5,000.

In one case the due date for the final payment is later than 31 January following the end of the year. If a taxpayer has notified chargeability by 5 October but the notice to file a tax return is not issued before 31 October, then the due date for the payment is three months after the issue of the notice.

Penalties for late payment of tax

Penalties for late payment of tax will be imposed in respect of balancing payments of income tax.

Paid	Penalty
(a) Within 30 days of due date:	none
(b) Not more than six months after the due date:	5% of unpaid tax
(c) More than six months but not more than twelve months after the due date:	a further 5%
(d) More than twelve months after the due date:	a further 5%

Penalties for late payment of tax apply to balancing payments of income tax. They do not apply to late payments on account.

Interest

INTEREST is chargeable on late payment of both payments on account and balancing payments. In both cases interest runs from the due date until the day before the actual date of payment.

If a taxpayer claims to reduce his payments on account and there is still a final payment to be made, interest is normally charged on the payments on account as if each of those payments had been the lower of:

(a) the reduced amount, plus 50% of the final income tax liability; and

(b) the amount which would have been payable had no claim for reduction been made

HOW IT WORKS

Harry made two payments on account of £2,500 each for 2011/12. The payments were made on 31 January 2012 and 31 July 2012. Harry had claimed to reduce these payments from the £4,000 that would have been due had they been based on his previous year's income tax liability.

Harry's 2011/12 tax return showed that his income tax liability for 2011/12 (before deducting payments on account) was £10,000. Harry paid the balance of income tax due of £5,000 on 30 September 2013.

Harry will be charged interest as follows:

The payments on account should have been £4,000 each. Interest will therefore be charged on the £1,500 not paid on 31 January 2012, from that date until the day before payment (29 September 2013). Similarly, interest will run on the other £1,500 that should have been paid on 31 July 2012 and was not paid until 30 September 2013.

The final balancing payment should have been £2,000 (£10,000 – £8,000). Interest will run on £2,000 from the due date of 31 January 2013 until the day before payment 29 September 2013.

Note. There would also be a late payment penalty of 10% due on the actual balancing payment of £5,000 (more than 6 months late).

Repayment of tax and repayment supplement

Tax is repaid when claimed unless a greater payment of tax is due in the following 30 days, in which case it is set-off against that payment.

Repayment supplement, ie interest, is paid on overpayments of:

(a) Payments on account
(b) Final payments of income tax
(c) Penalties

Repayment supplement runs from the later of the date of overpayment or the date the tax was due until the day before the tax is repaid. Tax deducted at source is treated as if it had been paid on the 31 January following the end of the tax year.

ENQUIRIES

HMRC can enquire into a return if it gives written notice within one year of:

(a) The actual filing date (if the return was filed on or before the due filing date)

(b) 31 January, 30 April, 31 July or 31 October following the actual filing date (if the return was filed after the due filing date)

A reason for raising an enquiry does not have to be given. In particular, the taxpayer will not be advised whether he has been selected at random for an audit. Enquiries may be full enquiries, or may be limited to 'aspect' enquiries.

In the course of the enquiries the taxpayer may be required to produce documents, accounts or other information. The taxpayer can appeal against this.

HMRC must issue a notice that enquiries are complete, and a statement of the amount of tax that should be included in the tax return, or the amount of a claim. The taxpayer then has 30 days to amend his return or claim to give effect to the conclusions. Alternatively, if the taxpayer is not satisfied he may, within 30 days, appeal.

Once an enquiry is complete, further enquiries cannot be made.

CHAPTER OVERVIEW

- A tax return must be filed by 31 January following a tax year provided it is filed online. Paper returns must be filed by 31 October following the tax year
- A penalty may be imposed if the taxpayer makes an error in his tax return based on the Potential Loss of Revenue as a result of the error
- A penalty may be imposed if the taxpayer does not notify HMRC of his liability to pay income tax or capital gains tax. The penalty is based on Potential Lost Revenue.
- A fixed penalty of £100 applies if a return is filed late; followed by a daily penalty of £10 if the return is filed between three and six months late
- A tax-geared penalty may apply if a return is filed more than six months late, with a further penalty if this is over twelve months late
- Payments on account of income tax are required on 31 January in the tax year and on 31 July following the tax year
- Balancing payments of income tax are due on 31 January following the tax year
- Late payment penalties apply to balancing payments of income tax. They do not apply to late payments on account
- Interest is chargeable on late payment of both payments on account and balancing payments
- HMRC can enquire into a return, usually within one year of receipt of the return

Keywords

Filing due date – the date by which a return must be filed

Payment on account – an amount paid on account of income tax

Interest – charged on late payments on account and on late balancing payments

Repayment interest – payable by HMRC on overpaid payments on account, balancing payments and penalties

TEST YOUR LEARNING

Test 1

What is the due filing date for an income tax return for 2011/12 assuming the taxpayer will submit the return online?

Test 2

How will 2011/12 payments on account be calculated and when are they due?

Test 3

A notice requiring a tax return for 2011/12 is issued in April 2012 and the return is filed online in May 2013. All income tax was paid in May 2013. No payments on account were due. What charges will be made on the taxpayer?

Test 4

Susie filed her 2011/12 tax return online on 28 January 2013. By what date must HMRC give notice that they are going to enquire into the return?

A 31 January 2014
B 31 March 2014
C 6 April 2014
D 28 January 2014

Test 5

Jamie paid income tax of £12,000 for 2010/11. In 2011/12, his tax payable was £16,000.

State when payments must be made in respect of Jamie's 2011/12 income tax liability and the amounts due.

Test 6

Tim should have made two payments on account of his 2011/12 income tax liability of £5,000 each. He actually made both of these payments on 31 August 2012.

State the amount of any penalties for late payment.

£	

Test 7

Lola accidentally fails to include an invoice of £17,000 on her 2011/12 tax return. She is a basic rate taxpayer, and has not yet disclosed this error. What is the maximum penalty that could be imposed on her?

A £5,100
B £3,400
C £1,020
D £2,380

chapter 9: COMPUTING TAXABLE TOTAL PROFITS

chapter coverage 🕮

In this chapter we see how to compute a company's taxable total profits for corporation tax. We also see that taxable total profits must be computed for accounting periods.

The topics that we shall cover are:

- ✍ Taxable total profits
- ✍ Long periods of account

TAXABLE TOTAL PROFITS

To arrive at the profits on which a company must pay tax you need to aggregate the company's various sources of income together with its chargeable gains. You should then deduct the amount of any Gift Aid donations paid. The resulting figure is known as the company's TAXABLE TOTAL PROFITS. The computation is shown in the following pro forma:

	£
Trading profits	X
Interest	X
Property business profits	X
Other income	X
Chargeable gains	X
Total profits	X
Less: Gift Aid donations paid	(X)
Taxable total profits	X

Dividends received from other companies are usually exempt from corporation tax and so not included in taxable total profits. You will not be expected to deal with non exempt UK dividends in your assessment.

We will now look at each of the items in the above pro forma in turn.

Trading profits

The trading profits of a company are, broadly, computed in the same way that the trading profits of a sole trader are computed. You should, therefore, take the net profit in the company's accounts and adjust it for tax purposes in the same way as you would adjust a sole trader's accounts profit. We looked at adjustment of profit earlier in this Text.

One important difference is in the calculation of capital allowances. There is never a private use asset column in a company's capital allowance computation. This is because there is never any reduction of allowances to take account of any private use of an asset. The director or employee suffers a taxable benefit instead.

Task 1

N Ltd makes up its accounts to 31 March each year. In the year to 31 March 2012, the income statement showed the following:

	£
Gross profit (note)	514,000
General expenses (all allowable)	(85,000)
Net profit	429,000

Note. Gross profit includes trading profit of £510,000 and property business income of £4,000.

The company had a main pool with a value of £21,500 as at 1 April 2011. On 1 December 2011, the company bought a car with CO_2 emissions of 140g/km for £11,000. The car was used by a director of the company. It was agreed that 20% of the use of the car was private use by the director.

(1) Using the pro forma layout provided, calculate the capital allowances available for the year to 31 March 2012.

Y/E 31 MARCH 2012	Main pool	Allowances
	£	£
B/f	21,500	
NON-AIA ADDITION – CAR	11,000	
	32,500	
WDA @ 20%	(6500)	6500
C/f	26,000	

(2) Using the pro forma layout provided, calculate the trading profits for the year to 31 March 2012.

	£
NET PROFIT	429,000
LESS: PROPERTY BUSINESS INCOME	(4000)
	425,000
LESS: CAPITAL ALLOWANCES	(6500)
TRADING PROFITS	418,500

(3) Using the pro forma layout provided, calculate the taxable total profits for the year to 31 March 2012.

	£
TRADING PROFITS	418,500
PROPERTY BUSINESS INCOME	4000
TAXABLE TOTAL PROFITS	422,500

Interest received

Companies receive non-trading interest gross from banks and building societies (ie no tax is deducted in advance from the amount received). Interest received from other companies (this includes debenture interest) is also received gross.

Interest paid

Companies may also pay interest for example on loans taken out by the company, including the issue of loan stock or debenture stock.

If the loan is for a trading purpose (eg to buy plant and machinery for use in the company's trade), the interest is deductible when computing the company's trading income.

If the loan is for a non-trading purpose (eg to buy investments such as shares or properties to rent out), the interest is deductible from non-trading interest received (eg from a bank or building society) to give a net figure to be used in computing taxable total profits. In some cases, there may be a deficit of non-trading interest paid over non-trading interest received, but the treatment of such a deficit is not in your syllabus.

Other costs of raising loan finance, such as fees, are dealt with in the same way as interest paid.

Property business income

A company with property business income must pool the rents and expenses on all of its properties, to give a single profit or loss. Property business income is taxed on an accruals basis.

You will not be expected to calculate property business income in your Business Tax assessment. However, you may be given a profit or loss figure and required to deal with it in the corporation tax computation as appropriate.

Chargeable gains

Companies do not pay capital gains tax. Instead their net chargeable gains (current period gains less current period losses) are brought into the computation of taxable total profits. Chargeable gains for companies are dealt with later in this Text.

Gift Aid donations

Charitable gifts of money qualify for tax relief under the Gift Aid scheme if they cannot be deducted as a trading expense.

For companies, Gift Aid donations paid are deducted in computing taxable total profits as shown in the pro forma above. They have to be paid ie not just accrued, in the accounting period, and the amount paid is the amount deducted (ie there is no grossing up for companies).

Sometimes a Gift Aid donation will have been deducted in computing the accounts profit. If this is the case, the amount deducted must be added back in computing taxable **trading** profits, and is then deducted when computing taxable total profits.

Income received/paid net of tax

Companies receive patent royalties from individuals net of 20% tax. This means that the individual withholds 20% tax and pays it over to HMRC on the company's behalf.

Income received net of tax is included within the corporation tax computation at its gross equivalent. For example £8,000 of patent royalties received net of tax would need to be grossed up by multiplying by 100/80 to include £10,000 within either trading profits or other income.

Patent royalties and interest paid by a company to individuals are paid net of 20% tax. It is the gross amount that is deducted in the corporation tax computation, either from trading profits or from interest or other income as described above.

Payments of royalties and interest by a company to a company are made gross and so there are no income tax implications.

HOW IT WORKS

ST Ltd draws up accounts for the year ended 31 March 2012 which show the following results:

		£	£
Gross profit on trading			180,000
Dividends received from other companies			7,900
Bank interest received			222
Profit on sale of investments			20,000
Less:	Trade expenses (all allowable)	83,400	
	Bank interest payable (overdraft)	200	
	Debenture interest payable (gross)	3,200	
	Payment to charity under Gift Aid	100	
	Depreciation	9,022	(95,922)
Profit before taxation			112,200

Notes

1 The capital allowances for the accounting period total £5,500.

2 The debentures were issued on 1 August 2011 to raise working capital. The £3,200 charged in the accounts represents six months interest (£2,400) paid and two months accrued;

3 The profit on the sale of investments resulted in a chargeable gain of £13,867.

The calculation of the company's taxable total profits is as follows:

		£	£
Net profit per accounts			112,200
Less:	dividends received	7,900	
	profit on investments	20,000	
	interest received	222	
			(28,122)
			84,078
Add:	Gift Aid payment	100	
	depreciation	9,022	
			9,122
			93,200
Less:	capital allowances		(5,500)
Trading profits			87,700
Interest received			222
Chargeable gain			13,867
			101,789
Less:	Gift Aid payment		(100)
Taxable total profits			101,689

Note. The dividends received from other companies are not included within taxable total profits.

Task 2

A company had the following results in the year ended 31 March 2012.

	£
Trading profits	85,000
Bank deposit interest income	6,000
Building society interest income	1,500
Dividends received	3,200
Capital gains	2,950
Gift Aid donation paid	15,200

The company's taxable total profits are:

£	

LONG PERIODS OF ACCOUNT

A PERIOD OF ACCOUNT is the period for which a company prepares its accounts.

An ACCOUNTING PERIOD is the period for which corporation tax is charged.

A company's accounting period is often the same as its period of account. However, an accounting period cannot be longer than twelve months. This means that if a period of account exceeds 12 months, it must be divided into two accounting periods: the first will comprise the first 12 months and the second will comprise the balance. It is necessary to prepare separate computations of taxable total profits for each accounting period.

The following rules are applied in apportioning income, gains and Gift Aid donations between accounting periods:

(a) Trading income (before deducting capital allowances) is apportioned on a time basis;

(b) Capital allowances and balancing charges are calculated separately for each accounting period;

(c) Property business income is apportioned on a time basis as applies for trading income;

(d) Interest income on non-trading loans is allocated to the period in which it accrues;

(e) Other income is apportioned on a time basis;

(f) Chargeable gains are allocated to the accounting period in which the disposal takes place;

(g) Gift Aid donations are allocated to the accounting period in which they are paid.

The apportionment rules are illustrated in the following example.

HOW IT WORKS

Beta Ltd makes up its accounts for a 15 month period ended 31 March 2012. Trading income is £150,000 for the 15 month period. No capital allowances were due for the period.

Bank deposit interest of £672 was credited on 31 March 2011 and £1,402 on 31 March 2012. The amounts accrued at 1 January 2011 and 1 January 2012 were £412 and £950 respectively.

The company made a payment of £3,630 under the Gift Aid scheme on 14 March 2011.

Disposals of chargeable assets realised a chargeable gain of £5,300 on 14 March 2011 and a chargeable gain of £807 on 14 March 2012.

The company's taxable total profits are as follows:

	Note	AP 1.1.11 – 31.12.11	AP 1.1.12 – 31.3.12
		£	£
Trading income (12/15:3/15)	1	120,000	30,000
Interest	W	1,210	452
Chargeable gains	2	5,300	807
Less: Gift Aid	3	(3,630)	–
Taxable total profits		122,880	31,259

Notes

1 Trading income is time apportioned.

2 Chargeable gains are allocated to the period in which the relevant disposal takes place.

3 Gift Aid donations are allocated to the period in which they are paid.

Working

Interest income is allocated to the period in which it accrued as follows:

	12m to 31.12.11	**3m to 31.3.12**
	£	£
Bank interest credited	672	1,402
Less: opening accrual	(412)	(950)
Add: closing accrual	950	–
Amount accrued	1,210	452

Task 3

X Ltd makes up a 15 month set of accounts to 30 June 2012 with the following results.

	£
Trading profits	300,000
Interest 15 months @ £500 accruing per month	7,500
Capital gain (1 May 2011 disposal)	250,000
Less: Gift Aid donation (paid 31.12.11)	(50,000)
	507,500

Using the pro forma layout provided, calculate the taxable total profits for each of the accounting periods based on the above accounts.

	12 MONTH ended 31/3	3 MONTHS ended 30/6
	£	£
TRADING PROFITS	240,000	60,000
INTEREST	6000	1500
CAPITAL GAIN	250,000	–
LESS: GIFT AID	(50,000)	–
TAXABLE TOTAL PROFITS	446,000	61,500

CHAPTER OVERVIEW

- Adjustment of profit for companies is similar to that for individuals but there is no private use adjustment
- To compute taxable total profits aggregate all sources of income and chargeable gains. Deduct Gift Aid donations
- Patent royalties and interest are received/paid to individuals net of 20% tax. Include the gross amounts in the computation of taxable total profits
- An accounting period cannot exceed 12 months in length
- A long period of account must be split into two accounting periods: a period of 12 months and then a period covering the balance of the period of account

Keywords

Taxable total profits – The profits on which a company must pay corporation tax

Period of account – The period for which a company prepares its accounts

Accounting period – The period for which corporation tax is charged

TEST YOUR LEARNING

Test 1

In computing taxable total profits, how much would be included in respect of the following items (actual amount received):

	Type of income	Amount received	Amount to be included
(1)	building society interest	£6,000	6000
(2)	bank deposit interest	£3,900	3900
(3)	dividends from other companies	£9,000	0
(4)	patent royalties received from an individual	£6,000	7500

There were no amounts accrued at the beginning or end of the year.

Test 2

A company shows the following accrued amount (gross) for interest for the year ended 31 March 2012:

Interest payable = £4,000

The interest payable was paid on a loan taken out to buy some machinery for use in the company's trade.

How will this be treated in the corporation tax computation?

A Added to compute trading income

B Added to compute net non-trading interest

(C) Deducted to compute trading income

D Deducted to compute net non-trading interest

Test 3

On 30 June 2011, Edelweiss Ltd makes a donation to Help the Aged of £385. The donation was made under the Gift Aid scheme.

The deduction available in respect of the charitable donation when calculating taxable total profits is:

Test 4

X Ltd had been making up accounts to 31 May for several years. Early in 2011 the directors decided to make accounts to 31 August 2011 (instead of 31 May 2011) and annually thereafter to 31 August. The two chargeable accounting periods for CT purposes will be:

A	1 June 2010 – 31 March 2011	and	1 April 2011 – 31 August 2011
(B)	1 June 2010 – 31 May 2011	and	1 June 2011– 31 August 2011
C	1 June 2010 – 31 December 2010	and	1 January 2011 – 31 August 2011
D	1 June 2010 – 31 August 2010	and	1 September 2010 – 31 August 2011

Test 5

C Ltd prepares accounts for the 16 months to 30 April 2012. The results are as follows:

	£
Trading profits	320,000
Bank interest received (accrued evenly over period)	1,600
Chargeable gain (made 1.1.12)	20,000
Gift Aid donation (paid 31.12.11)	15,000

Using the pro forma layout provided, calculate the taxable total profits for the accounting periods based on the above results.

	1/1/11 - 31/12/11	1/1/12 - 30/4/12
	£	£
TRADING PROFITS	240,000	80,000
BANK INTEREST	1200	400
CHARGEABLE GAIN	—	20,000
LESS: GIFT AID DONATION	(15,000)	—
	226,200	100,400

chapter 10: COMPUTING CORPORATION TAX PAYABLE

chapter coverage

In this chapter we see how to compute the corporation tax that a company must pay on its taxable total profits. We start by looking at single companies with 12 month accounting periods. We then consider the effect of short accounting periods and the effect of a company being associated with other companies. Finally, we look at the marginal rate of tax that applies when a company has profits between certain limits.

You will also be introduced to the pages of the corporation tax return that you may have to complete in your assessment.

The topics that we shall cover are:

- Determining augmented profits
- Computing the corporation tax liability
- Short accounting periods
- Associated companies
- The marginal rate of tax
- Company tax return form

DETERMINING AUGMENTED PROFITS

Corporation tax rates are fixed for financial years. A FINANCIAL YEAR runs from 1 April to the following 31 March and is identified by the calendar year in which it begins.

For example, the year ended 31 March 2012 is the Financial Year 2011 (FY 2011). This should not be confused with a tax year, that runs from 6 April to the following 5 April.

The corporation tax rate for any particular Financial Year depends on the level of a company's augmented profits. Augmented profits are taxable total profits plus the grossed-up amount of dividends received from other companies. The grossed-up amount of a dividend received is the dividend received grossed up by multiplying by 100/90. The exception to this is dividends received from associated companies that are not taken into account in a calculation of augmented profits.

HOW IT WORKS

A company had taxable total profits of £400,000 in the year ended 31 March 2012. In this year it received dividends of £9,000.

Augmented profits are:

	£
Taxable total profits	400,000
Dividend (£9,000 × 100/90)	10,000
Augmented profits	410,000

Task 1

A company had taxable total profits of £60,000 and dividends received of £4,500 in the year to 31 December 2011. The company's augmented profits for the year were:

£	

COMPUTING THE CORPORATION TAX LIABILITY

In this section we look at how to compute corporation tax for a twelve month accounting period where the company does not have associated companies. We will look at other situations later in this chapter.

To work out the CT rate that applies, augmented profits have to be compared with various limits. These limits will be given to you in the tax rates and allowances tables in the assessment.

The main rate of corporation tax

The main rate of corporation tax (CT) for Financial Year 2011 is 26%.

If a company's augmented profits exceed the upper limit for Financial Year 2011, the main rate of corporation tax is charged for the year. For the Financial Year 2011, the upper limit is £1,500,000.

HOW IT WORKS

A Ltd had the following results in the year to 31 March 2012:

Taxable total profits £1,450,000
Dividend received £90,000

Augmented profits for the year are £1,450,000 + (£90,000 × 100/90) = £1,550,000

As augmented profits are above the upper limit, the main rate of corporation tax applies.

Corporation tax due is £1,450,000 × 26% = £377,000.00

Note that although augmented profits are used to determine the **rate** of CT, CT is only charged on taxable total profits.

Task 2

For the year to 31 March 2012, M Ltd had the following results:

	£
Taxable total profits	2,100,000
Dividend received	45,000

M Ltd's corporation tax liability for the year is:

£	546000		00

2,100,000
50,000
2,150,000

Marginal relief

Marginal relief applies where the augmented profits of an accounting period are between the lower and upper limits. For Financial Year 2011 these limits are £300,000 and £1,500,000.

To calculate corporation tax, first calculate the corporation tax at the main rate on taxable total profits and then deduct:

(U – A) × N/A × standard fraction

where U = upper limit (currently £1,500,000)
A = augmented profits
N = taxable total profits

The standard fraction is 3/200 for FY 2011.

You will be given the marginal relief formula and the standard fraction in the tax rates and allowances tables in the assessment.

HOW IT WORKS

B Ltd has the following results for the year ended 31 March 2012:

	£
Taxable total profits	280,000
Dividend received 1 December 2011	45,000

First, calculate augmented profits to determine the rate of corporation tax:

	£
Taxable total profits	280,000
Dividends received (45,000 x 100/90)	50,000
Augmented profits	330,000

As augmented profits are between the lower and upper limits, marginal relief applies:

	£
Taxable total profits £280,000 @ 26%	72,800.00
Less: 3/200 £(1,500,000 – 330,000) × $\frac{280,000}{330,000}$	(14,890.91)
Corporation tax payable	57,909.09

Task 3

For the year to 31 March 2012, M Ltd, has the following results:

	£
Trading profits	220,000
Dividend received	90,000

(1) Using the pro forma layout provided, calculate the augmented profits of M Ltd for the year to 31 March 2012.

	£
TAXABLE TOTAL PROFITS	220,000
DIVIDENDS RECEIVED (90,000 × 100/90)	100,000
AUGMENTED PROFITS	320,000

(2) Using the pro forma layout provided, calculate the corporation tax liability of M Ltd for the year to 31 March 2012.

	£
TAXABLE TOTAL PROFITS £220,000 @ 26%	57.200
LESS (1,500,000 - 320,000) × 220,000/320,000 × 3/200	(12,168.75)
1,180,000 × .6875	45,031.25

Small profits rate (SPR)

The SPR of corporation tax (20% for FY 2011) applies to the taxable total profits of companies whose augmented profits are below the lower limit. For FY 2011 this limit is £300,000.

HOW IT WORKS

X Ltd had the following results for the year ended 31 March 2012:

	£
Taxable total profits	100,000
Dividend received	18,000

First calculate augmented profits:

	£
Taxable total profits	100,000
Dividend received (× 100/90)	20,000
Augmented profits	120,000

As augmented profits are below £300,000, the small profits rate of tax is applied to taxable total profits.

CT payable 20% × £100,000 = £20,000.00

Task 4

BD Ltd had the following results for the year to 31 March 2012:

Taxable total profits = £60,000

No dividends were received in the year.

The corporation tax liability for the year is:

Periods straddling FY10 and FY11

The main rate of CT for FY 2010 is 28%.

The SPR for FY 2010 is 21%.

There is no change to the limits of £300,000 and £1,500,000.

However, as there is a change in the corporation tax rates between these two Financial Years, they will need to be dealt with separately when calculating a company CT liability.

HOW IT WORKS

Claude Ltd makes up accounts to 30 September each year. For the year ended 30 September 2011 it had taxable total profits of £1,800,000. It received dividends of £216,000.

The first step is to work out the augmented profits to decide whether the small profits rate, marginal relief or the main rate should apply.

Augmented profits are £1,800,000 + £216,000 × $\frac{100}{90}$ = £2,040,000

This means the main rate of CT applies.

The second step is then to decide the number of months that fall into FY10 and the number of months that fall into FY11 and apportion the taxable total profits accordingly.

With the year ended 30 September 2011, six months of the accounting period falls in FY10 (1 October 2010 to 31 March 2011) and six months falls into FY11 (1 April 2011 to 30 September 2011).

The third step is then to apply the correct rate of corporation tax to the separate apportioned taxable total profits for the corresponding FY.

Tax on taxable total profits (FY10)

£1,800,000 x 6/12 × 28% = £252,000.00

Tax on taxable total profits (FY11)

£1,800,000 x 6/12 × 26% = £234,000.00

Therefore total CT liability for year ended 30 September 2011 is £486,000.00

Task 5

Frances Ltd makes up accounts to 31 December each year. For the year ended 31 December 2011 its income statement (profit and loss account) was as follows.

	£
Taxable total profits	240,000
Dividends plus tax credits	50,000
Augmented profits	290,000

The corporation tax liability for the year is:

£			

SHORT ACCOUNTING PERIODS

We have seen above how to compute a corporation tax liability for a 12 month accounting period. If an accounting period lasts for less than 12 months the lower and upper limits discussed above are reduced proportionately.

HOW IT WORKS

For the six months to 31 October 2011 L Ltd had taxable total profits of £40,000 and no dividends received. Compute the corporation tax payable.

First, work out augmented profits as usual:

	£
Taxable total profits	40,000
Dividends received	0
Augmented profits	40,000

Next compare this with the lower limit applicable in the short accounting period:

Lower limit £300,000 × 6/12 = £150,000

As augmented profits are below the lower limit the small profits rate of tax applies:

CT liability (FY11) £40,000 × 20% = £ 8,000.00

Note: All six months fell into FY11, so there was no need to apportion the taxable total profits.

If the accounting period is short, and the augmented profits fall between the time-apportioned (ie the reduced) upper and lower limits, marginal relief will apply. In the marginal relief calculation, the upper limit used is the reduced upper limit.

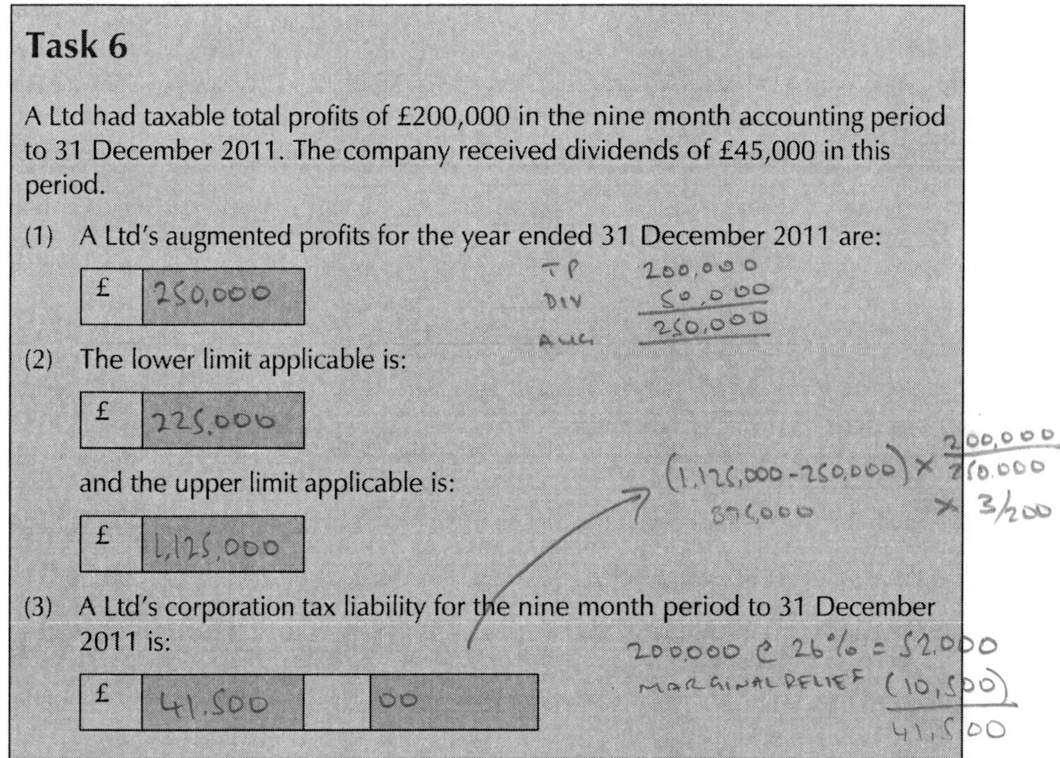

Task 6

A Ltd had taxable total profits of £200,000 in the nine month accounting period to 31 December 2011. The company received dividends of £45,000 in this period.

(1) A Ltd's augmented profits for the year ended 31 December 2011 are:

£

(2) The lower limit applicable is:

£

and the upper limit applicable is:

£

(3) A Ltd's corporation tax liability for the nine month period to 31 December 2011 is:

£

ASSOCIATED COMPANIES

The expression ASSOCIATED COMPANY in tax has no connection with financial accounting.

For tax purposes a company is associated with another company if it either controls the other or if both are under the control of the same person or persons (individuals, partnerships or companies).

If a company has one or more 'associated companies', then the upper and lower limits are divided by the number of associated companies + 1 (for the company itself).

Companies that have only been associated for part of an accounting period are deemed to have been associated for the whole period for the purpose of determining these limits.

An associated company is ignored for these purposes if it has not carried on any trade or business at any time in the accounting period (or the part of the period during which it was associated). This means that you should ignore dormant companies. However, you should include non UK companies.

When working out augmented profits any dividends received from associated companies are ignored. You should assume dividends received are not from associated companies unless specifically told otherwise.

HOW IT WORKS

For the year to 31 March 2012, T Ltd, a company with one associated company, has the following results:

	£
Taxable total profits	330,000
Dividend received	45,000

First compute augmented profits

	£
Taxable total profits	330,000
Dividends £45,000 × 100/90	50,000
Augmented profits	380,000

Next compare augmented profits to the lower and upper limits:

Lower limit	£300,000/2	= £150,000
Upper limit	£1,500,000/2	= £750,000

The limits are divided by two as there are two companies that are associated with each other.

As augmented profits are between these limits, marginal relief applies:

FY11	£
£330,000 × 26%	85,800.00
Less: Small profits marginal relief	
$3/200\ £(750,000 - 380,000) \times \frac{330,000}{380,000}$	(4,819.74)
	80,980.26

As in the case of limits reduced for a short accounting period, the upper limit used in the marginal relief calculation is the reduced upper limit.

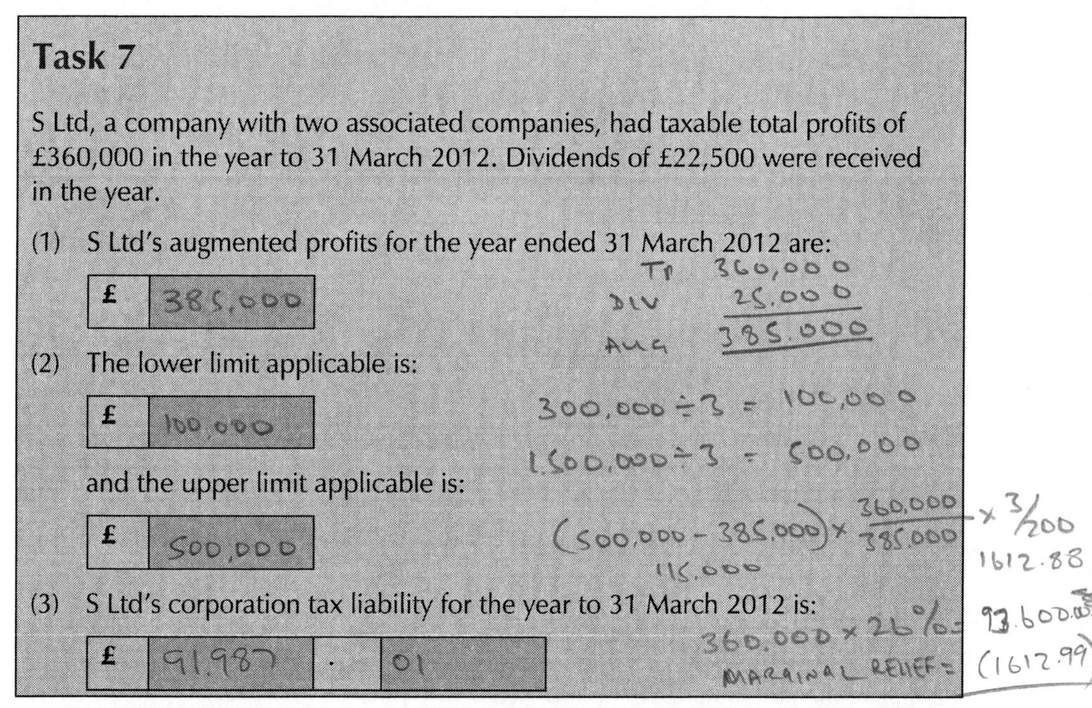

Task 7

S Ltd, a company with two associated companies, had taxable total profits of £360,000 in the year to 31 March 2012. Dividends of £22,500 were received in the year.

(1) S Ltd's augmented profits for the year ended 31 March 2012 are:

£

(2) The lower limit applicable is:

£

and the upper limit applicable is:

£

(3) S Ltd's corporation tax liability for the year to 31 March 2012 is:

£ .

THE MARGINAL RATE OF TAX

In your assessment you may need to be aware that there is a marginal rate of tax of 27.5% for FY11 that applies to taxable total profits between the upper and lower limits.

This is calculated as follows:

	£		£
Upper limit	1,500,000	@ 26%	390,000
Lower limit	(300,000)	@ 20%	(60,000)
Difference	1,200,000		330,000

$$\frac{330,000}{1,200,000} = 27.5\%$$

Effectively any taxable total profits (here £1,200,000) falling between the upper and lower limits is taxed at a rate of 27.5%

HOW IT WORKS

S Ltd has taxable total profits of £350,000 for the year ended 31 March 2012. Its corporation tax liability is:

		£
£350,000 × 26%		91,000.00
Less:	Small profits marginal relief	
	3/200 £(1,500,000 – 350,000)	(17,250.00)
		73,750.00

This is the same as calculating tax at:

20% × £300,000 + 27.5% × £50,000 = £60,000 + £13,750 = £73,750

Consequently tax is charged at an effective rate of 27.5% on taxable total profits that exceeds the lower limit, up to the upper limit.

Note that although there is an effective corporation tax charge of 27.5%, this rate of tax is never used in actually calculating corporation tax. The rate is just an effective marginal rate that you must be aware of.

It may be important to consider the effective rate of tax suffered by a company when you are deciding how best to relieve losses. However, you do not need to remember how to perform the above computations calculating the marginal rate.

COMPANY TAX RETURN FORM

In your assessment you may be asked to complete the company tax return. A copy of the tax calculation page is available at the end of this chapter. You will be able to practise completing this form in the Business Tax Question Bank.

CHAPTER OVERVIEW

- The rate of corporation tax due in a Financial Year depends on the level of a company's augmented profits
- Augmented profits need to be compared with the upper and lower limits to determine the appropriate rate
- Tax may be due at the main rate or the small profits rate. Marginal relief applies when augmented profits are between the upper and lower limits
- Reduce the limits proportionately in short accounting periods
- Divide the limits by the number of associated companies + 1 (for the company itself)
- As corporation tax rates changed between FY10 and FY11 there is a need to split a year straddling 31 March 2011 when calculating the corporation tax liability.

Key words

A Financial Year – runs from 1 April to the following 31 March and is identified by the calendar year in which it begins

Augmented profits – are taxable total profits plus the grossed-up amount of dividends received from other (non associated) companies

A company is associated – with another company if either controls the other or if both are under the control of the same person or persons (individuals, partnerships or companies)

TEST YOUR LEARNING

Test 1

S Ltd, a company with no associated companies, had taxable total profits of £255,000 for its six month accounting period to 31 March 2012. No dividends were paid or received in the period.

Its corporation tax liability for the period will be:

A £47,625.00
B £51,000.00
C £58,875.00
D £66,300.00

Test 2

G Ltd, a company with no associated companies, made up accounts for the nine month period to 31 December 2011. The augmented profits for this period were £55,000, including £5,000 of gross dividends.

The corporation tax liability for the period is:

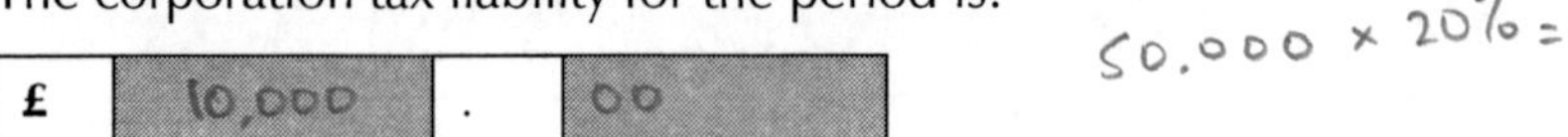

Test 3

J Ltd, a company with no associated companies, had taxable total profits of £90,000 in the year ended 31 December 2011. No dividends were received in the year.

The corporation tax liability for the year is:

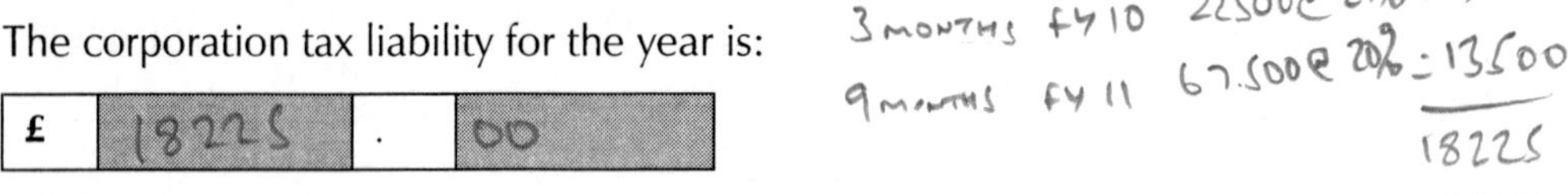

Test 4

S Ltd, a company with one associated company, had taxable total profits of £180,000 for the nine month period to 31 March 2012.

Its corporation tax liability for the year will be:

A £38,250.00
B £32,625.00
C £41,062.50
D £46,800.00

Test 5

VAC Ltd, a company with no associated companies, has taxable total profits for the year to 31 March 2012 of £750,000.

What is the marginal rate of corporation tax paid by the company on its profits between £300,000 and £750,000?

A 20%
B 23%
C 26%
D 27.5%

Test 6

True/false: Financial Year 2011 begins on 1 April 2011 and ends on 31 March 2012.

Page 2

Company tax calculation

Turnover

1 Total turnover from trade or profession — 1 £

Income

3 Trading and professional profits — 3 £

4 Trading losses brought forward claimed against profits — 4 £

5 Net trading and professional profits — box 3 minus box 4 — 5 £

6 Bank, building society or other interest, and profits and gains from non-trading loan relationships — 6 £

11 Income from UK land and buildings — 11 £

14 Annual profits and gains not falling under any other heading — 14 £

Chargeable gains

16 Gross chargeable gains — 16 £

17 Allowable losses including losses brought forward — 17 £

18 Net chargeable gains — box 16 minus box 17 — 18 £

21 Profits before other deductions and reliefs — sum of boxes 5, 6, 11, 14 & 18 — 21 £

Deductions and Reliefs

24 Management expenses under S75 ICTA 1988 — 24 £

30 Trading losses of this or a later accounting period under S393A ICTA 1988 — 30 £

31 *Put an 'X' in box 31 if amounts carried back from later accounting periods are included in box 30* — 31

32 Non-trade capital allowances — 32 £

35 Charges paid — 35 £

37 Profits chargeable to corporation tax — box 21 minus boxes 24, 30, 32 and 35 — 37 £

Tax calculation

38 Franked investment income — 38 £

39 Number of associated companies in this period — 39

or

40 Associated companies in the first financial year — 40

41 Associated companies in the second financial year — 41

42 *Put an 'X' in box 42 if the company claims to be charged at the starting rate or the small companies' rate on any part of its profits, or is claiming marginal rate relief* — 42

Enter how much profit has to be charged and at what rate of tax

Financial year *(yyyy)*	Amount of profit	Rate of tax	Tax
43	44 £	45	46 £ p
53	54 £	55	56 £ p

63 Corporation tax — total of boxes 46 and 56 — 63 £ p

64 Marginal rate relief — 64 £ p

65 Corporation tax net of marginal rate relief — 65 £ p

66 Underlying rate of corporation tax — 66 • %

67 Profits matched with non-corporate distributions — 67

68 Tax at non-corporate distributions rate — 68 £ p

69 Tax at underlying rate on remaining profits — 69 £ p

70 Corporation tax chargeable — *See note for box 70 in CT600 Guide* — 70 £ p

CT600 (Short) (2008) Version 2

chapter 11: CHARGEABLE GAINS FOR COMPANIES

chapter coverage

In this chapter we look at the rules which apply to the computation of chargeable gains for companies.

We start by considering when a chargeable gain arises and then how to compute gains and losses for companies. We will cover gains and losses for individuals later in this Text.

We then look at some special rules for part disposals and chattels.

The topics that we shall cover are:

- When does a chargeable gain arise?
- Computing chargeable gains and allowable losses for companies
- Part disposals
- Chattels

WHEN DOES A CHARGEABLE GAIN ARISE?

For the gain on the disposal of a capital asset to be a chargeable gain there must be a CHARGEABLE DISPOSAL of a CHARGEABLE ASSET by a CHARGEABLE PERSON.

Chargeable persons

Individuals and companies are the only type of chargeable persons that you will meet in Business Tax.

Chargeable disposals

The following are the most important chargeable disposals:

- Sales of assets or parts of assets
- Gifts of assets or parts of assets

A chargeable disposal occurs on the date of the contract (where there is one, whether written or oral), or the date of a conditional contract becoming unconditional.

Chargeable assets

All assets are chargeable assets unless they are specifically designated as exempt.

The following are the exempt assets that you need to be aware of:

- Motor vehicles suitable for private use
- Gilt-edged securities (for individuals only)
- Certain chattels (see later in this Chapter)

Any gain arising on disposal of an exempt asset is not taxable and any loss is not allowable.

The exempt asset most commonly appearing in assessment tasks is a car. You should not waste time computing a gain or loss on a car. All you need to do is state that the car is an exempt asset, so no gain or loss arises.

Remember that sales of assets as part of the trade of a business (ie sales of inventory) give rise to trading profits and not chargeable gains.

COMPUTING CHARGEABLE GAINS AND ALLOWABLE LOSSES FOR COMPANIES

Whenever a chargeable asset is disposed of by a company, a calculation to determine the amount of any gain or loss is needed. The computation follows a standard format as shown below:

	£
Disposal consideration (or market value)	100,000
Less: incidental costs of disposal	(1,000)
Net proceeds	99,000
Less: allowable costs	(28,000)
Less: enhancement expenditure	(1,000)
Unindexed gain/allowable loss	70,000
Less: indexation allowance	(10,000)
Chargeable gain	60,000

We will now look at each of the items in the above pro forma in turn.

Disposal consideration

Usually the disposal consideration is the proceeds of sale of the asset, but a disposal is deemed to take place at market value:

(a) Where the disposal is by way of a gift
(b) Where the disposal is made for a consideration which cannot be valued
(c) Where the disposal is made to a connected person (see later in this Text)

Costs

The following costs are deducted in the above pro forma:

(a) **Incidental costs of disposal**

These are the costs of selling an asset. They may include advertising costs, estate agents fees, legal costs or valuation fees. These costs should be deducted separately from any other allowable costs.

(b) **Allowable costs**

These include:

(i) The original purchase price of the asset

(ii) Costs incurred in purchasing the asset (estate agents fees, legal fees etc)

(c) **Enhancement expenditure**

ENHANCEMENT EXPENDITURE is capital expenditure which enhances the value of the asset and is reflected in the state or nature of the asset at the time of disposal.

Indexation allowance

Indexation was introduced to remove the inflationary element of a gain from taxation.

Companies are entitled to an indexation allowance from the date the expenditure was incurred until the date of disposal of the asset.

HOW IT WORKS

M Ltd bought a shop for use in his business on 12 June 1989 and sold it on 1 March 2012.

Indexation allowance is available for the period June 1989 to March 2012.

To calculate an indexation allowance, you need an indexation factor calculated from the month the asset was acquired to the month the asset was sold. You will be given this indexation factor in the assessment. You will not be expected to calculate it.

The indexation factor is multiplied by the cost of the asset (including costs of acquisition) to calculate the indexation allowance.

Similarly, indexation is available on enhancement expenditure incurred. This expenditure is multiplied by an indexation factor that runs from the month the expenditure was incurred to the month of sale.

Indexation allowance does not apply to incidental costs of disposal.

HOW IT WORKS

K Ltd bought an asset on 19 August 1991 for £10,000. Enhancement expenditure of £1,000 was incurred on 12 June 2003. The asset is sold for £41,500 on 20 February 2012. The disposal costs were £1,500.

Calculate the chargeable gain arising on the sale of the asset. Assume indexation factors: August 1991 to February 2012 = 0.799; June 2003 to February 2012 = 0.308.

	£
Disposal consideration	41,500
Less: incidental costs of disposal	(1,500)
Net proceeds	40,000
Less: purchase price	(10,000)
Less: enhancement expenditure	(1,000)
	29,000
Less: indexation on purchase price	
£10,000 × 0.799	(7,990)
indexation on enhancement expenditure	
£1,000 × 0.308	(308)
Chargeable gain	20,702

Task 1

L Ltd bought a freehold factory in July 2000 for £80,000. It sold the factory for £200,000 in August 2011. Assume indexation factor July 2000 – August 2011 = 0.366.

Complete the following computation:

Proceeds	200,000
Cost	(80,000)
Indexation allowance 80,000 × ·366	(29,280)
Gain	90,720

The indexation allowance cannot create or increase an allowable loss. If there is a gain before the indexation allowance, the allowance can reduce that gain to zero, but no further. If there is a loss before the indexation allowance, there is no indexation allowance.

Task 2

S plc bought an asset for £50,000 in August 1994 and sold it for £20,000 in January 2012. Assume an indexation factor August 1994 – January 2012 = 0.624.

The allowable loss is:

20,000
(50,000)
(30,000)

£	(30,000)

Task 3

T plc bought an asset for £50,000 in August 1994 and sold it for £70,000 in January 2012. Assume an indexation factor August 1994 – January 2012 = 0.624.

The gain/ loss is:

£	

PART DISPOSALS

Sometimes part, rather than the whole, of an asset is disposed of. For instance, one-third of a piece of land may be sold. In this case, we need to be able to compute the chargeable gain or allowable loss arising on the part of the asset disposed of.

The problem is that although we know what the disposal proceeds are for the part of the asset disposed of, we do not usually know what proportion of the cost of the whole asset relates to that part. The solution to this is to use the following fraction to determine the cost of the part disposed of.

The fraction is:

$$\frac{A}{A+B}=\frac{\text{Value of the part disposed of}}{\text{Value of the part disposed of} + \text{Market value of the remainder}}$$

A is the proceeds (or market value) before deducting incidental costs of disposal.

You must learn the above formula for use in your exam.

The formula is used to apportion the cost of the whole asset. If, however, any expenditure was incurred wholly in respect of the part disposed of, it should be treated as an allowable deduction in full for that part and not apportioned. An example of this is incidental selling expenses, which are wholly attributable to the part disposed of.

HOW IT WORKS

Z Ltd bought four acres of land for £270,000 to hold as an investment. It sold one acre of the land at auction for £200,000, before auction expenses of 15%. The market value of the three remaining acres is £460,000. The indexation factor applicable is 0.850.

The cost of the land being sold is:

$$\frac{200{,}000}{200{,}000+460{,}000}\times £270{,}000 = £81{,}818$$

	£
Disposal proceeds	200,000
Less: incidental costs of sale (15%)	(30,000)
Net proceeds	170,000
Less: cost (see above)	(81,818)
	88,182
Less: indexation allowance £81,818 x 0.850	(69,545)
Chargeable gain	18,637

Task 4

Y Ltd bought a plot of land for investment purposes for £100,000 in July 2002. In January 2012, it sold part of the land for net proceeds of £391,000, after legal fees on the sale of £9,000. At that time, the value of the remaining land was £600,000. The indexation factor between July 2002 and January 2012 is 0.324.

(1) The cost of the part of the land sold is:

£	

(2) The chargeable gain arising on the disposal is:

£	

CHATTELS

A CHATTEL is tangible moveable property (ie property that can be moved, seen and touched). Examples are items such as furniture and works of art.

A WASTING CHATTEL is a chattel with an estimated remaining useful life of 50 years or less. An example would be a racehorse or a greyhound. Wasting chattels are exempt from CGT (so that there are no chargeable gains and no allowable losses). There is one exception to this, being plant and machinery used in the taxpayer's trade, but this will not be tested in your assessment.

Task 5

A Ltd bought a racehorse for £36,000. The horse was sold for £40,000.

True/False: a chargeable gain of £4,000 arises on the disposal.

There are special rules for calculating gains and losses on non-wasting chattels:

(a) If a chattel is not a wasting asset, any gain arising on its disposal will still be exempt from CGT if the asset is sold for gross proceeds of £6,000 or less

(b) If sale proceeds exceed £6,000, but the cost is less than £6,000 the gain is limited to:

5/3 × (gross proceeds – £6,000)

(c) If sale proceeds are less than £6,000, any allowable loss is restricted to that which would arise if it were sold for gross proceeds of £6,000

We will have a look at examples of each of these situations in turn.

HOW IT WORKS

P Ltd purchased a painting for £3,000 in February 2010. In January 2012 it sold the painting at auction. The indexation factor between February 2010 and January 2012 is 0.086.

If the gross sale proceeds are £4,000, the gain on sale will be exempt.

If the gross proceeds are £8,000 with costs of sale of 10%, the gain arising on the disposal of the painting will be calculated as follows:

	£
Gross proceeds	8,000
Less: incidental costs of sale (10%)	(800)
Net proceeds	7,200
Less: cost	(3,000)
	4,200
Less: indexation allowance £3,000 × 0.086	(258)
Chargeable gain	3,942
Gain cannot exceed 5/3 × £(8,000 – 6,000)	£3,333

Task 6

J plc purchased a non-wasting chattel for £2,500 in August 2008. On 1 October 2011 it sold the chattel at auction for £10,000 (which was then subject to auctioneer's commission at 5%). The indexation factor between August 2008 and October 2011 is 0.095.

The gain arising is:

A nil

B £6,762

C £6,667

D £5,833

HOW IT WORKS

M Ltd purchased an antique desk for £8,000. It sold the desk in an auction for £4,750 net of auctioneer's fees of 5%.

M Ltd obviously has a loss and therefore the allowable loss is calculated on deemed proceeds of £6,000. The costs of disposal can be deducted from the deemed proceeds of £6,000.

	£
Deemed disposal proceeds	6,000
Less: incidental costs of disposal (£4,750 × 5/95)	(250)
	5,750
Less: cost	(8,000)
Allowable loss	(2,250)

Task 7

Q plc purchased a non-wasting chattel for £8,800 which it sold at auction for £3,600 (which was net of 10% commission). The allowable loss is:

£	

CHAPTER OVERVIEW

- A chargeable gain arises when there is a chargeable disposal of a chargeable asset by a chargeable person
- Enhancement expenditure can be deducted in computing a chargeable gain if it is reflected in the state and nature of the asset at the time of disposal
- The indexation allowance gives relief for the inflation element of a gain
- On the part disposal of an asset, the formula A/(A + B) must be applied to work out the cost attributable to the part disposed of
- Wasting chattels are exempt assets for CGT purposes (eg racehorses and greyhounds)
- Gains on non-wasting chattels are exempt if they are sold for gross proceeds of £6,000 or less. If gross proceeds exceed £6,000 any gain arising on the disposal of the asset is limited to 5/3 (gross proceeds – £6,000)
- If the gross proceeds are less than £6,000 on the sale of a non-wasting chattel, any loss otherwise arising is restricted by deeming the gross proceeds to be £6,000

Keywords

Chattel – tangible moveable property

Wasting chattel – a chattel with an estimated remaining useful life of 50 years or less

TEST YOUR LEARNING

Test 1

Indexation allowance runs from DATE EXPENDITURE to DATE OF DISPOSAL. Fill in the blanks.

Test 2

J plc bought a plot of land in July 2002 for £80,000. It spent £10,000 on drainage in April 2005. It sold the land for £200,000 in August 2011. Assume indexation factors July 2002 – August 2011 = 0.301 and April 2005 – August 2011 = 0.214.

Using the pro forma layout provided, compute the gain on sale.

	£
PROCEEDS SALE	200,000
LESS: COST	(80,000)
LESS: ENHANCEMENT	(10,000)
	110,000
LESS: INDEXATION ON COST	(24080)
LESS: " ON ENHANCEMENT	(2140)
CHARGEABLE GAIN	83780

Test 3

X Ltd bought four acres of land for £50,000 in December 2006. In February 2012, it sold one acre of the land for £80,000. At the time of the sale, the value of the three remaining acres was £120,000. The indexation factor between December 2006 and February 2012 is 0.188.

(1) The cost of the part of the land sold is:

$\frac{80,000}{80,000+120,000} \times 50,000$

£	20,000

(2) The chargeable gain arising on the disposal is:

£	56,240

80,000
(20,000)
60,000
(3760)
56240

Test 4

M plc purchased a non-wasting chattel for £3,500 in August 2009. In October 2011 it sold the chattel at auction for £8,000. The indexation factor between August 2009 and October 2011 is 0.045.

The gain arising is:

£	3333

8000
(3500)
4500.00
INDEX (157.50)
4342.50

$5/3 \times (8000 - 6000)$

Test 5

S Ltd bought a non-wasting chattel for £8,700 in October 2005. It sold the chattel for £4,300 in May 2011. The indexation factor between October 2005 and May 2011 is 0.186.

The allowable loss on sale is:

A £(6,018)
B £(4,400)
C £(2,700)
D £(4,318)

chapter 12: SHARE DISPOSALS BY COMPANIES

chapter coverage 📖

In this chapter we consider the rules which apply when a company disposes of shares in another company.

The topics that we shall cover are:

- ✍ Why special rules are needed for shares
- ✍ Matching rules
- ✍ The FA 1985 pool
- ✍ Bonus issues and rights issues

WHY SPECIAL RULES ARE NEEDED FOR SHARES

Shares present special problems when computing gains or losses on disposal. For instance, suppose that A plc buys some shares in X plc on the following dates:

	No of shares	*Cost*
		£
5 July 1991	100	150
17 January 1996	100	375
2 July 2011	100	1,000

On 15 July 2011, A plc sells 220 of the shares it owns in X plc for £3,300. To work out A plc's chargeable gain, we need to be able to identify which shares out of the three holdings were actually sold. Since one share is identical to any other, it is not possible to work this out by reference to factual evidence.

As a result, it has been necessary to devise 'matching rules'. These allow us to identify on a disposal which shares have been sold and so work out what the allowable cost (and therefore the gain) on disposal should be. These matching rules are considered in detail below.

It is very important that you understand the matching rules. These rules are very regularly examined and if you do not understand them you will not be able to get any of this part of a question right.

MATCHING RULES

For companies the matching of shares sold is in the following order.

(a) Shares acquired on the same day

(b) Shares acquired in the previous nine days (if more than one acquisition, on a 'first in, first out' basis - FIFO)

(c) Shares from the FA 1985 which is a pool of other share acquisitions

The composition of the FA 1985 pool is explained in more detail below.

There is no indexation allowance on shares acquired in the previous nine days, even if the acquisition is in the previous month to the disposal.

HOW IT WORKS

Z Ltd acquired the following shares in L plc:

Date of acquisition	*No of shares*
9 November 2003	15,000
15 December 2005	15,000
11 July 2011	5,000
15 July 2011	5,000

Z Ltd disposed of 20,000 of the shares on 15 July 2011.

We match the shares as follows.

(a) acquisition on same day: 5,000 shares acquired 15 July 2011.

(b) acquisitions in previous 9 days: 5,000 shares acquired 11 July 2011.

(c) FA 1985 share pool: 10,000 shares out of 30,000 shares in FA 1985 share pool (9 November 2003 and 15 December 2005)

Task 1

B Ltd acquired shares in J plc as follows:

Date of acquisition	No. of shares
9 October 2005	1,000
11 June 2007	1,500
12 July 2011	1,200

B Ltd sold 2,000 on 15 July 2011.

The disposal will be matched with:

A 1,000 shares acquired on 9 October 2005, then with 1,000 shares acquired on 11 June 2007

B 2,000 shares from the acquisitions in 2005 and 2007 in the FA 1985 pool

C 2,000 shares from the acquisitions in 2005, 2007 and 2011 in the FA 1985 pool

D 1,200 shares acquired on 12 July 2011, then with 800 shares in the FA 1985 pool

THE FA 1985 POOL

The FA 1985 pool comprises the following shares:

(a) Shares held by a company on 1 April 1985 and acquired by that company on or after 1 April 1982.

(b) Shares acquired by that company on or after 1 April 1985.

We must keep track of:

(a) the number of shares
(b) the cost of the shares ignoring indexation
(c) the indexed cost of the shares

For historical reasons, your first step with a FA 1985 pool should be to compute its value at 1 April 1985. To do this aggregate the indexed cost and number of shares acquired between April 1982 and 1 April 1985 . In order to calculate the indexed cost of these shares, an indexation allowance, computed from the date of acquisition of the shares to April 1985, is added to the cost value.

HOW IT WORKS

J Ltd bought 10,000 shares in X plc for £6,000 in August 1982 and another 10,000 for £9,000 in December 1984. Indexation factors are August 1982 – April 1985 0.157, December 1984 – April 1985 0.043.

Compute the value of the FA 1985 pool at 6 April 1985.

	No of shares	*Cost*	*Indexed cost*
		£	£
August 1982 (a)	10,000	6,000	6,000
December 1984 (b)	10,000	9,000	9,000
	20,000	15,000	15,000
Index to April 1985			
£6,000 × 0.157 (a)			942
£9,000 × 0.043 (b)			387
Pool at 5 April 1985	20,000	15,000	16,329

Your second step should be to reflect all disposals and acquisitions of shares in the FA 1985 pool between 1 April 1985 and ten days before the disposal. Disposals/acquisitions of shares that decrease/increase the amount of expenditure within the FA 1985 pool are called OPERATIVE EVENTS.

You must reflect each operative event in the FA 1985 pool. However, prior to reflecting an operative event within the FA 1985 share pool, a further indexation allowance (sometimes described as an indexed rise) must be computed up to the date of the operative event you are looking at. You must look at each operative event in chronological order.

HOW IT WORKS

Following on from the above example, now assume that J Ltd acquired 4,000 more shares on 1 January 1990 at a cost of £6,000.

Show the value of the FA 1985 pool on 1 January 1990 following the acquisition. Assume an indexation factor April 1985 – January 1990 0.261.

	No of shares	*Cost*	*Indexed cost*
		£	£
6 April 1985	20,000	15,000	16,329
Index to January 1990			
0.261 × £16,329			4,262
			20,591
January 1990 acquisition	4,000	6,000	6,000
	24,000	21,000	26,591

If there are several operative events, the procedure described must be performed several times over. In the case of a disposal, following the calculation of the indexed rise, the cost and the indexed cost attributable to the shares disposed of are deducted from the cost and the indexed cost within the FA 1985 pool. This is computed on a pro-rata basis if only part of the holding is being sold.

HOW IT WORKS

Continuing the above example, suppose that J Ltd now disposes of 12,000 shares on 9 January 2012 for £26,000.

Show the value of the FA 1985 pool on 10 January 2012 following the disposal. Compute the gain on the disposal. Assume an indexation factor January 1990 – January 2012 0.921.

	No of shares	Cost	Indexed cost
		£	£
Value at January 1990	24,000	21,000	26,591
Indexed rise to January 2012 0.921 × £26,591			24,490
	24,000	21,000	51,081
Disposal	(12,000)	(10,500)	(25,541)
Pool c/f	12,000	10,500	25,540

The gain on the disposal is calculated as follows:

	£
Sale proceeds	26,000
Less: cost	(10,500)
	15,500
Less: indexation (£25,541 – £10,500)	(15,041)
Gain	459

Note that the indexation is the difference for the shares sold between the indexed cost and the cost.

Task 2

W Ltd acquired and disposed of shares in Z plc as follows:

No of shares	Date	Cost
		£
3,000	10 August 2002	9,000
10,000	25 April 2004	45,000
(1,000)	13 September 2007	–
(8,500)	24 November 2011	–

The proceeds of sale of the shares sold on 24 November 2011 were £47,200.

(1) Using the pro forma layout provided, show the share pool of W Ltd. Assume the following indexation factors:

August 2002 – April 2004	0.041
April 2004 – September 2007	0.104
September 2007 – November 2011	0.137

	No of shares	*Cost*	*Indexed cost*
		£	£
10 AUG 2002	3000	9000	9000
INDEX TO APRIL 2004			369
25 APR 2004	10,000	45,000	45,000
C/F	13,000	54,000	54,369
INDEX TO SEP 2007			5654
			60,023
DISPOSAL 13 SEP 2007	(1000)	(4154)	(4617)
C/F	12,000	49846	55406
INDEX TO NOV 2011			7591
			62,997
DISPOSAL 24 NOV 2011	(8500)	(35,308)	(44,623)
C/F	3500	14,538	18,374

(2) Calculate the gain on sale in November 2011.

	£
PROCEEDS	47,200
COST	(35,308)
	11,892

LESS INDEXATION (44623 − 35,308) (9315)

GAIN 2577

BONUS ISSUES AND RIGHTS ISSUES

Bonus issue

A BONUS ISSUE is where additional shares are given free to shareholders based on their current holdings. Sometimes this is done when shares become quite expensive and so less easy to trade. For example, where a share in a company is worth £20, it might be better from a trading point of view to have 4 shares worth £5 each. The company could issue 3 bonus shares for each one share owned (a 3 for 1 bonus issue). The overall value of each shareholder's holding will not change as a result of the bonus issue but the value of each share will be reduced.

Bonus shares are treated as being acquired at the date of the original acquisition of the underlying shares giving rise to the bonus issue.

Since bonus shares are issued at no cost there is no need to adjust the original costs. Instead the number of shares purchased at particular times are increased by the bonus issue. There is no need to index the FA 1985 pool to the date of the bonus issue as this is not classed as an 'operative event'. The normal matching rules apply.

Rights issue

A RIGHTS ISSUE is where shareholders in a company are offered the right to buy new shares in that company based on their current holdings. A company may do this if it wants to raise extra capital. The rights shares may be offered at a discount to the market value to encourage shareholders to take up the offer rather than buying shares from other shareholders as this does not benefit the company.

The difference between a bonus issue and a rights issue is that in a rights issue the new shares are paid for. This results in an adjustment to the original cost.

Rights shares are treated as being acquired at the date of the original acquisition of the underlying shares giving rise to the rights issue. Therefore, rights shares derived from shares in the FA 1985 pool go into that holding. You should add the number and cost of each rights issue to each holding as appropriate. This is important to remember if you are looking at rights issue shares acquired and then disposed of within nine days. The nine day rule will not apply to these shares as they will be treated for matching purposes as having been acquired on original date of acquisition of the underlying shares.

However, for the purposes of calculating the indexation allowance for rights issues, expenditure on a rights issue is taken as being incurred on the date of the issue and not on the acquisition date of the original holding. Therefore the FA 1985 pool needs to be indexed to the date of the rights issue as this is classed as an 'operative event'.

HOW IT WORKS

S Ltd had the following transactions in the shares of B Ltd

May 1987	Purchased 2,000 shares for £4,000
May 2001	Took up one for two rights issue at £2.00 per share
October 2011	Sold all the shares for £14,000

Compute the chargeable gain or allowable loss arising on the sale in October 2011.

Indexation factors: May 1987 – May 2001 = 0.745; May 2001 – October 2011 = 0.330

	No of shares	*Cost*	*Indexed cost*
		£	£
May 1987	2,000	4,000	4,000
Indexed rise to May 2001			
£4,000 × 0.745			2,980
			6,980
Rights issue	1,000	2,000	2,000
	3,000	6,000	8,980
Indexed rise to October 2011			
£8,980 × 0.330			2,963
	3,000	6,000	11,943

	£
Disposal proceeds	14,000
Less Cost	(6,000)
Less indexation (£11,943 – £6,000)	(5,943)
Chargeable gain	2,057

Task 3

S Ltd bought 10,000 shares in T plc in May 2001 at a cost of £45,000.

There was a 2 for 1 bonus issue in October 2003.

There was a 1 for 3 rights issue in June 2007 at a cost of £4 per share. S Ltd took up all of its rights entitlement.

S Ltd sold 20,000 shares in T plc for £120,000 in January 2012.

The indexed rise between May 2001 and June 2007 is 0.163 and between June 2007 and January 2012 is 0.156.

(1) Using the pro forma layout provided, show the share pool.

	No of shares	*Cost*	*Indexed cost*
		£	£
ACQUISITION MAY 2001	10,000	45,000	45,000
BONUS ISSUE OCT 2003	20,000		
	30,000		
INDEXED RISE JUN 2007			7335
RIGHTS ISSUE JUN 2007	10,000	40,000	40,000
	40,000	85000	92335
INDEXED RISE JAN 2012			14,404
			106739
DISPOSAL JAN 2012	(20,000)	(42,500)	(53,370)
C/F	20,000	42,500	53,369

(2) The gain on sale is:

£	66630

PROCEEDS 120,000
COST (42,500)
77500
INDEX (53,370 − 42,500) (10,870)
66630

CHAPTER OVERVIEW

- There are special rules for matching shares sold by a company with shares purchased.
- Disposals are matched with acquisitions on the same day, the previous nine days (FIFO basis) and the FA 1985 share pool
- In the FA 1985 share pool, we must keep track of the number of shares, the cost of the shares and the indexed cost
- Operative events increase or decrease the amount of expenditure within the FA 1985 pool
- Bonus issue shares are acquired without payment
- Rights issue shares are acquired for payment but are treated as acquired at the same time as the original holding, except that indexation allowance is calculated from the date of payment

Key words

Operative events – are events, disposals/acquisitions of shares that decrease/increase the amount of expenditure within the FA 1985 pool

Bonus issue – is where shares are issued free to shareholders based on original holdings

Rights issues – are similar to bonus issues except that in a rights issue shares must be paid for

TEST YOUR LEARNING

Test 1

What are the share matching rules for company shareholders?

SAME DAY
PREVIOUS 9 DAY (FIFO)
FA1985 POOL

Test 2

Q Ltd bought 10,000 shares in R plc in May 2001 at a cost of £90,000. There was a 1 for 4 rights issue in June 2007 at the cost of £12 per share and Q Ltd took up all of its rights entitlement.

The indexed rise between May 2001 and June 2007 is 0.163 and between June 2007 and January 2012 is 0.156.

Q Ltd sold 10,000 shares in R plc for £150,000 in January 2012.

(1) Using the pro forma layout provided, show the share pool.

		No of shares	*Cost*	*Indexed cost*
MAY 2001	ACQUISITION	10,000	90,000	90,000
JUN 2007	INDEXED RISE ·163			14,670
JUNE 2007	RIGHTS ISSUE 1 FOR 4	2500	30,000	30,000
		12500	120,000	134,670
JAN 2012	INDEXED RISE ·156			21,009
		12,500	120,000	155,679
JAN 2012	DISPOSAL	(10,000)	(96,000)	(124,543)
C/F		2,500	24,000	31,136

(2) Using the pro forma layout provided, compute the gain on sale.

	£
PROCEEDS	150,000
COST	(96,000)
	54,000
INDEXED (124,543 - 96,000)	(28,543)
	25,457

chapter 13: CORPORATION TAX LOSSES

chapter coverage

In this chapter we look at the methods by which a company may obtain relief for any trading losses it incurs. We also look at how relief may be obtained for various non-trading losses.

The topics that we shall cover are:

- Relieving trading losses
- Relief against future trading income
- Relief against total profits
- Relieving non-trading losses
- Choosing loss relief

RELIEVING TRADING LOSSES

You need to be aware of the following three methods by which a company may obtain relief for its trading losses:

(a) carry forward against future trading profits;
(b) set-off against current profits;
(c) carry back against earlier profits.

We will look at each of these three methods of obtaining loss relief below.

When doing tasks involving corporation tax losses it is useful to have a standardised layout. Your answer should be divided into two parts – the taxable profits for each period and a loss memorandum. The examples in this session show the most convenient way of laying out your answer.

RELIEF AGAINST FUTURE TRADING INCOME

A company can claim to set a trading loss against profits from the same trade in future accounting periods. Relief is given against the first available trading profits. This relief is called CARRY FORWARD LOSS RELIEF.

HOW IT WORKS

P Ltd has the following results for the three years to 31 March 2012:

	Year ended 31 March		
	2010	***2011***	***2012***
	£	£	£
Trading profit/(loss)	(8,000)	3,000	6,000
Bank interest	0	4,000	2,000

Carry forward loss relief would be relieved as follows:

	Year ended 31 March		
	2010	***2011***	***2012***
	£	£	£
Trading profit	NIL	3,000	6,000
Less: carry forward loss relief	–	(3,000) (i)	(5,000) (ii)
Bank interest	–	4,000	2,000
Taxable total profits	NIL	4,000	3,000

Loss memorandum

	£
Loss for year ended 31 March 2010	8,000
Loss carried forward at 1 April 2010	8,000
Loss relief year ended 31 March 2011	(3,000) (i)
Loss carried forward at 1 April 2011	5,000
Loss relief year ended 31 March 2012	(5,000) (ii)
Loss carried forward at 1 April 2012	NIL

Note that the carried forward loss is set against the trading profits only in future years. It cannot be set against other income such as the bank interest.

Task 1

On 1 April 2011 M Ltd had the following amount brought forward:

Trading losses	£50,000

M Ltd's results for the year to 31 March 2012 were:

	£
Trading profits	40,000
Property business income	25,000
Capital gain	2,000

(1) The taxable total profits for the year to 31 March 2012 are:

£

(2) What amount, if any, of the trading losses remain to be carried forward at 1 April 2012?

£

RELIEF AGAINST TOTAL PROFITS

A company may claim to offset a trading loss incurred in an accounting period against total profits (before deducting Gift Aid donations) of the same accounting period. This relief is called CURRENT PERIOD LOSS RELIEF.

A trading loss that cannot be fully relieved against profits of the same accounting period may be carried back and usually relieved against total profits of the twelve months immediately preceding the loss making period. This relief is called CARRY

BACK LOSS RELIEF. Current period relief must be used in the loss making period before carry back loss relief.

Where the loss is being carried back it is set against profits before the deduction of Gift Aid donations. Any Gift Aid donations that become unrelieved, as a result of a carry back claim, are lost.

Claims for current period or carry back loss cannot specify how much of the loss is to apply and, once made, must relieve profits to the maximum possible extent.

Any loss remaining unrelieved after current period and carry back loss relief claims must be carried forward and set against future profits of the same trade under carry forward loss relief.

HOW IT WORKS

Patagonia Ltd started trading on 1 August 2009 and has the following results for the first two accounting periods to 31 July 2011:

	Year ended 31 July	
	2010	***2011***
	£	**£**
Trading profit (loss)	45,000	(50,000)
Building society interest	400	5,300
Gift Aid	500	500

Current period and carry back loss relief would be relieved as follows:

	Year ended 31 July	
	2010	***2011***
	£	**£**
Trading profit	45,000	–
Interest	400	5,300
	45,400	5,300
Less: current period loss relief	–	(5,300)
	45,400	–
Less: carry back loss relief	(44,700)	–
Less: Gift Aid	(500)	–
Taxable total profits	200	NIL
Unrelieved Gift Aid donations	–	500

Loss memorandum

		£
Loss incurred in year ended 31 July 2011		50,000
Less:	current period loss relief	
	(year ended 31 July 2011)	(5,300)
		44,700
Less:	carry back loss relief	
	12 months to 31 July 2010	(44,700)
Loss carried forward		NIL

Task 2

JB Ltd had the following results in the three accounting periods to 31 March 2013:

	Year ended 31 March 2011	Year ended 31 March 2012	Year ended 31 March 2013
	£	£	£
Trading profits/(loss)	70,000	(160,000)	60,000
Property income	10,000	10,000	10,000
Gift Aid donation	(10,000)	(30,000)	(15,000)

Using the pro forma layout provided, show how the trading loss of £160,000 incurred in the year to 31 March 2012 may be relieved. Clearly show any Gift Aid donations which become unrelieved and any losses to carry forward.

	Year ended 31 March 2011	Year ended 31 March 2012	Year ended 31 March 2013
	£	£	£
TRADING PROFIT	70,000	—	60,000
PROPERTY INCOME	10,000	10,000	10,000
	80,000	10,000	70,000
LESS CURRENT PERIOD	—	(10,000)	—
	80,000	—	70,000
LESS BACK PERIODS	(80,000)	—	
	—		
LESS FORWARD RELIEF	—	—	(60,000)
			10,000
LESS GIFT AID	(10,000)	(30,000)	(15,000)
UNRELIEVED	10,000	30,000	5000

LOSS C/F 10,000

The carry back loss relief is strictly a 12 month carry back. Therefore if the accounting period before the one of the loss is less than 12 months long, the loss can be carried back to the period before the short period. However, the profits available for relief in that period must be apportioned (on a time basis) to ensure that only 12 months of profits in total have had losses relieved against them.

RELIEVING NON-TRADING LOSSES

Capital losses

Capital losses are set against current year capital gains, and any remaining losses are carried forward and set against future gains. Capital losses can only be set against gains, never against income, and they cannot be carried back.

The following Task includes an example of the use of capital losses.

Task 3

Y Ltd had the following results for the three years to 31 October 2011:

	Year ended 31 October		
	2009	*2010*	*2011*
	£	£	£
Trading profits/(loss)	50,000	40,000	(90,000)
Bank interest	10,000	5,000	5,000
Chargeable gain/(allowable loss)	(7,000)	–	12,000

Using the pro forma layout provided, calculate taxable total profits for each year assuming the company makes claims for loss relief against total profits.

	Year ended 31 October		
	2009	*2010*	*2011*
	£	£	£
TRADING PROFIT	50,000	40,000	—
BANK INTEREST	10,000	5,000	5000
CHARGEABLE GAIN (12,000-7000)	—	—	5000
TOTAL PROFITS	60,000	45,000	10,000
CURRENT PERIOD RELIEF	—	—	(10,000)
CARRY BACK RELIEF		(45,000)	
TOTAL TAXABLE PROFITS	60000	NIL	NIL

C/F LOSS £35,000

Property business losses

Property business losses are first set off against other income and gains of the company for the current period.

Any excess is then carried forward as a property business loss as if it had arisen in the later accounting period for offset against future income (of all descriptions).

CHOOSING LOSS RELIEF

Several alternative loss reliefs may be available. In making a choice consider:

(a) The rate at which relief will be obtained:

- (i) 26% at the main rate
- (ii) 20% at the small profits rate
- (iii) 27.5% if marginal relief applies

We previously outlined how the 27.5% marginal rate is calculated. Remember this is just a marginal rate of tax; it is never actually used in computing a company's corporation tax.

(b) How quickly relief will be obtained: loss relief against total profits is quicker than carry forward loss relief.

(c) The extent to which relief for Gift Aid donations might be lost.

CHAPTER OVERVIEW

- Trading losses may be carried forward and set against future trading profit of the same trade
- Current period loss relief is available in the loss making period
- Carry back loss relief is set against profits in the previous 12 months
- Current period and carry back relief is given against total profits before deducting Gift Aid donations
- A claim for current period loss relief must be made before a loss is carried back
- Capital losses can be set against capital gains of the same or future accounting periods
- Property business losses are first set-off against other income and gains of the current period and any excess is carried forward as a rental loss in the next period
- When selecting a loss relief, consider the rate at which relief is obtained and the timing of the relief

Keywords

Carry forward loss relief – allows a company to set a trading loss against profits from the same trade in future accounting periods

Current period loss relief – allows a trading loss to be set against total profits before deducting Gift Aid donations in the loss making accounting period

Carry back loss relief – allows a trading loss to be set against total profits, before deducting Gift Aid donations, in the 12 months before the loss making period

TEST YOUR LEARNING

Test 1

(1) CR Ltd has the following results for the two years to 31 October 2011:

	Year ended 31 October	
	2010	***2011***
	£	**£**
Trading profit (loss)	170,000	(320,000)
Interest	5,000	60,000
Capital gain (loss)	(20,000)	12,000
Gift Aid payment	5,000	5,000

What amount of trading losses remain to be carried forward at 1 November 2011 assuming that all possible loss relief claims against total profits are made?

(2) What amount of capital loss remains to be carried forward at 1 November 2011?

Test 2

JB Ltd had the following results in the three accounting periods to 30 September 2011:

	Year ended 31 March 2010	*Six months to 30 September 2010*	*Year ended 30 September 2011*
	£	**£**	**£**
Trading profit/(loss)	4,000	6,000	(10,000)
Gift Aid donation	1,000	3,000	1,500

What amount, if any, of the trading loss incurred in the year ended 30 September 2011 may be relieved against total profits in the year ended 31 March 2010?

A £NIL
B £2,000
C £4,000
D £6,000

chapter 14: SELF ASSESSMENT FOR COMPANIES

chapter coverage 🕮

In this chapter we look at when corporation tax returns must be filed, for how long records must be kept and at the penalties chargeable for failure to comply with the requirements.

We then look at the due dates for payment of corporation tax and the consequences of late payment.

The topics that we shall cover are:

- Notification of chargeability
- Company tax returns and keeping records
- Payment of tax and interest

NOTIFICATION OF CHARGEABILITY

A company must notify HMRC when it first comes within the scope of corporation tax. This will usually be when it starts trading. There is a list of information that needs to be included in the notice, which must be given in writing. The notice must be made within three months.

The rules on penalties for late notification by taxpayers discussed earlier in this Text also apply to companies in relation to corporation tax.

COMPANY TAX RETURNS AND KEEPING RECORDS

A company that does not receive a notice requiring a corporation tax return (Form CT 600) to be filed must, if it is chargeable to tax, notify HMRC within twelve months of the end of the accounting period concerned. There is a penalty for late notification calculated in the same way as for late notification for individual taxpayers (see earlier in this Text). An obligation to file a return arises only when the company receives a notice requiring a return.

A return for each of the company's accounting periods is due on or before the FILING DUE DATE. This is the normally the later of:

(a) 12 months after the end of the period of account concerned, and

(b) three months from the date on which the notice requiring the return was made.

Companies are required to file their tax returns online, except in exceptional cases.

Task 1

Size Ltd prepares accounts for the twelve months to 30 September 2011. A notice requiring a CT600 return for the year ended 30 September 2011 was issued on 1 June 2012. The date by which Size Ltd must file its corporation tax return for the year to 30 September 2011 is

You saw earlier in this Text that if a period of account is more than twelve months long, there will be two accounting periods based on the period of account. The first accounting period is twelve months long, the second is for the remainder of the period of account.

A tax return must be filed for each accounting period. The tax returns for both accounting periods must be filed within twelve months of the end of the period of account.

Task 2

Ocado Ltd prepares accounts for the eighteen months to 30 June 2011.

The two accounting periods relating to this period of account are:

and

The date by which Ocado Ltd must file its corporation tax returns based on this period of account, assuming a notice requiring the returns was issued shortly after the end of the period of account, is:

Penalties for late filing

The rules on penalties for late filing of returns as discussed earlier in this Text also apply to companies in relation to corporation tax.

Task 3

Box Ltd prepares accounts for the twelve months to 30 June 2011. Assume a notice requiring the return for the period was issued shortly after the end of the period of account. Box Ltd filed this return on 24 December 2012. The penalty for late filing is:

Records

Companies must keep records until the latest of:

(a) six years from the end of the accounting period
(b) the date any enquiries are completed
(c) the date after which enquiries may not be commenced

All business records and accounts, including contracts and receipts, must be kept.

If a return is demanded more than six years after the end of the accounting period, the company must keep any records that it still has until the later of the end of any enquiry and the expiry of the right to start an enquiry.

Failure to keep records can lead to a penalty of up to £3,000 for each accounting period affected.

Penalties for error

The rules on penalties for errors made by taxpayers discussed earlier in this Text also apply to companies in relation to corporation tax returns.

Enquiries

HMRC may enquire into a return, provided that they give written notice that they are going to enquire by a year after:

(a) the actual filing date (if the return is filed on or before the due filing date)

(b) the 31 January, 30 April, 31 July or 31 October next following the actual filing date (if the return is filed after the due filing date)

Only one enquiry may be made in respect of any one return.

HMRC may demand that the company produce documents. The company may appeal against a notice requiring documents to be produced.

If HMRC demand documents, but the company does not produce them, there is a penalty of £300. There is also a daily penalty of up to £60 per day, which applies for each day from the day after the imposition of the £300 penalty until the documents are produced.

An enquiry ends when HMRC give notice that it has been completed and make any resulting amendments to the return. The company then has 30 days in which it may appeal to the Tax Tribunal against HMRC's amendments.

Task 4

Green Ltd prepares accounts for the twelve months to 30 April 2012. The tax return for the year was filed on 31 March 2013. The date by which HMRC may commence an enquiry into the return based on these accounts is:

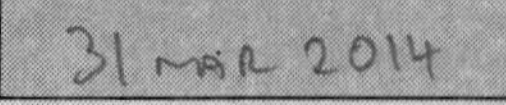

Task 5

A company has been making up its accounts annually to 31 May for many years. For the year ended 31 May 2010, it did not submit its corporation tax annual return (CT600) until 1 November 2011. A notice requiring the return was issued on 31 August 2010.

The latest date by which HMRC can commence an enquiry into the company's return is:

PAYMENT OF TAX AND INTEREST

Large companies

LARGE COMPANIES must pay their corporation tax in instalments. Broadly, a large company is any company that pays corporation tax at the main rate (profits exceed £1,500,000 where there are no associated companies).

Instalments are based on the estimated corporation tax liability of the company for the current period (not the previous period). This means that it is extremely important for companies to forecast their tax liabilities accurately. Large companies whose directors are poor at estimating may find their company incurring significant interest charges. The company must estimate its corporation tax liability in time for the first instalment, and must revise its estimate each quarter.

For a 12 month accounting period, quarterly instalments are due on the 14th day of months 7 and 10 in the accounting period and months 1 and 4 following the end of the period. You will not be expected to deal with periods other than 12 month periods in your assessment.

A company which draws up accounts to 31 December 2011 will pay instalments as follows:

Instalment	***Due date***
1	14 July 2011
2	14 October 2011
3	14 January 2012
4	14 April 2012

Task 6

S Ltd, a large company, has a corporation tax liability of £700,000 in respect of its accounting year 31 March 2012.

On which date will the company be required to pay its FINAL instalment of the liability?

A 14 October 2011
B 14 July 2012
C 31 July 2012
D 1 January 2013

Interest arises on late paid instalments (from the due date to the actual payment date (see below)). Interest is paid on overpaid instalments, from the actual payment date to the date of repayment, except that interest does not run before the due date for the first instalment. The position is looked at cumulatively after the due date for each instalment.

HOW IT WORKS

J Ltd makes up accounts to 31 December 2011. At the end of June 2011 it estimates that its total liability to corporation tax for the year will be £8m, all of which is due in instalments. The first instalment of £2m is paid on 14 July 2011.

In October 2011 the estimate of the corporation tax liability increases to £10m. A payment of £3m is made on 14 October 2011.

In November 2011 a chargeable gain is realised and thus an additional tax payment of £3.5m is made on 1 December 2011.

A third instalment of £5m is paid on 14 January 2012 and a final instalment of £2.5m is paid on 14 April 2012. The CT return shows a corporation tax liability of £16m for the year.

Summary

Tax Paid	***Instalment***	***Liability***
14 July 2011	£2m	£4m
14 October 2011	£3m	£4m
1 December 2011	£3.5m	–
14 January 2012	£5m	£4m
14 April 2012	£2.5m	£4m

Interest will be charged as follows:

Amount on which interest is charged	*Interest period*	*Note*
£2m	14 July – 13 October 2011	
£3m	14 October – 30 November 2011	
£(0.5)m	1 December 2011 – 13 January 2012	(1)
£(1.5)m	14 January – 13 April 2012	(1)

(1) Interest paid to company on overpayment of corporation tax.

Exceptions

If a 'small' company is treated as large as a result of the associated companies rule, it will not have to pay corporation tax by instalments if its own liability is less than £10,000.

If a company is a large company for an accounting period it will not have to pay corporation tax by instalments for that period if:

(a) its taxable total profits does not exceed £10m (reduced to reflect any associated companies at the end of the previous period); and

(b) it was not a large company in the previous year.

Incorrect instalments

There are penalties if a company deliberately and flagrantly fails to pay instalments of sufficient size. After a company has filed its return or HMRC has determined its liability, HMRC may wish to establish the reason for inadequate instalment payments. It can do this by asking the company to produce relevant information or records The failure to supply these will lead to an initial fixed penalty which may also be followed by a daily penalty which may continue until the information/records are produced.

Small and medium sized companies

Corporation tax is due for payment by small and medium sized companies nine months and one day after the end of the accounting period.

HOW IT WORKS

K Ltd makes up accounts to 31 March 2012. It is not a large company. The corporation tax for the year to 31 March 2012 is £30,000.

The corporation tax is due on 1 January 2013.

CHAPTER OVERVIEW

- A company must usually file its CT600 return within twelve months of the end of the period of account concerned
- Fixed penalties arise if the return is up to six months late. If the return is over six months late there may be a tax geared penalty
- Companies must normally keep records until six years after the end of the accounting period concerned
- HMRC can enquire into a return. Notice of an enquiry must usually be given within twelve months of the actual filing date.
- Large companies must pay their CT liability in 4 instalments starting in the 7th month of the accounting period. The final instalment is due in the fourth month following the end of the accounting period
- Small and medium sized companies must pay their corporation tax liability nine months and one day after the end of an accounting period

Keywords

The filing due date – is the date by which a tax return must be filed

Large companies – are companies that pay corporation tax at the main rate

TEST YOUR LEARNING

Test 1

A company has been preparing accounts to 30 June for many years. It submitted its CT600 return for the year to 30 June 2011 on 1 June 2012. By what date must HMRC give notice that they are going to commence an enquiry into the return?

Test 2

A company filed its CT600 return for the year to 31 December 2010 on 28 February 2012. What fixed penalty arises in respect of the late filing of the return for the year to 31 December 2010?

Test 3

Girton Ltd has no associated companies. When will the first payment of corporation tax be due on its taxable profits of £150,000 arising in the year ended 31 December 2011?

A 14 July 2011
B 1 October 2012
C 1 December 2012
D 1 January 2013

Test 4

Eaton Ltd has taxable total profits of £2,400,000 for its year ended 31 December 2012. The first instalment of the corporation tax liability for this year will be due on:

A 14 April 2012
B 14 April 2013
C 14 July 2012
D 1 October 2013

Test 5

M Ltd, a large company, has an estimated corporation tax liability of £240,000 in respect of its accounting year 31 March 2012.

What will be the amount of each of the company's quarterly instalments?

£

chapter 15: CHARGEABLE GAINS FOR INDIVIDUALS

chapter coverage 🕮

In this chapter we see how to compute chargeable gains or allowable losses arising on the disposal of assets by individuals.

We see how to set allowable losses against chargeable gains and how to arrive at the net gains taxable in any particular tax year. Then we note how to compute the capital gains tax payable in any particular tax year.

Finally, we look at the special rules that apply when disposals are made to connected people or between married couples/civil partners.

The topics covered are:

- Computing chargeable gains and allowable losses for individuals
- Part disposals
- Computing taxable gains in a tax year
- Computing capital gains tax payable
- Self assessment for capital gains tax
- Chattels
- Connected persons
- Spouses/civil partners

COMPUTING CHARGEABLE GAINS AND ALLOWABLE LOSSES FOR INDIVIDUALS

Whenever a chargeable asset is disposed of by an individual, a calculation to determine the amount of any gain or loss is needed. The computation follows a standard format as shown below:

	£
Disposal consideration (or market value)	100,000
Less: incidental costs of disposal	(1,000)
Net proceeds	99,000
Less: allowable costs	(28,000)
Less: enhancement expenditure	(1,000)
Chargeable gain/allowable loss	70,000

You will see that this is very similar to the computation of gains made by a company but there is no indexation allowance.

Task 1

Jack bought a holiday cottage for £25,000. He paid legal costs of £600 on the purchase.

Jack spent £8,000 building an extension to the cottage.

Jack sold the cottage for £60,000. He paid estate agent's fees of £1,200 and legal costs of £750.

Jack's gain on sale is:

£	

PART DISPOSALS

The same rules about part disposals which we looked at for company chargeable gains also apply to part disposals by individuals.

COMPUTING TAXABLE GAINS IN A TAX YEAR

An individual pays capital gains tax (CGT) on any TAXABLE GAINS arising in a tax year (6th April to 5th April).

Taxable gains are the net chargeable gains (gains minus losses) of the tax year reduced by unrelieved losses brought forward from previous years and the annual exempt amount. We will look at both of these items in turn.

Annual exempt amount

All individuals are entitled to an annual exempt amount. For 2011/12 it is £10,600. It is the last deduction to be made in computing taxable gains and effectively means that for 2011/12 the first £10,600 of chargeable gains are tax-free.

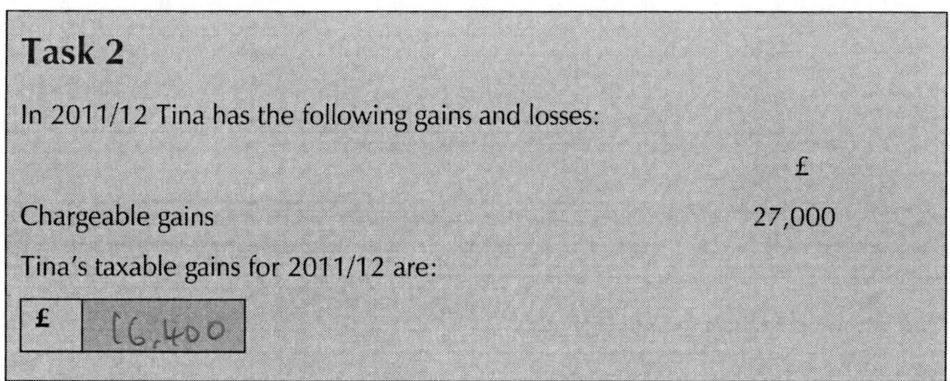

Task 2

In 2011/12 Tina has the following gains and losses:

	£
Chargeable gains	27,000

Tina's taxable gains for 2011/12 are:

£	16,400

Sometimes an allowable loss rather than a taxable gain arises. Once a loss has been calculated deal with it as follows:

(a) First, set it against gains arising in the same tax year until these are reduced to £Nil, then

(b) Set any remaining loss against net gains in the next tax year but only to reduce the net gains in the next year down to the annual exempt amount. Any loss remaining is carried forward.

HOW IT WORKS

(a) Tim has chargeable gains for 2011/12 of £25,000 and allowable losses of £16,000. As the losses are current year losses they must be fully relieved against the gains to produce net gains of £9,000, despite the fact that net gains are below the annual exempt amount.

(b) Hattie has gains of £11,000 for 2011/12 and allowable losses brought forward of £6,000. Hattie restricts her loss relief to £400 so as to leave net gains of £(£11,000 – £400) = £10,600, which will be exactly covered by the annual exempt amount for 2011/12. The remaining £5,600 of losses will be carried forward to 2012/13.

(c) Mildred has chargeable gains of £2,000 for 2011/12 and losses brought forward from 2010/11 of £12,000. She will leapfrog 2011/12 and carry forward all the brought forward losses to 2012/13. The gains of £2,000 are covered by the annual exempt amount for 2011/12.

Task 3

Sally had chargeable gains of £12,000 and allowable losses of £1,000 in 2011/12. She also had allowable losses of £3,000 brought forward from 2010/11. The capital losses carried forward to 2012/13 are:

A nil
B £4,000
C £3,000
D £2,600

COMPUTING CAPITAL GAINS TAX PAYABLE

The rate at which CGT is payable depends on whether the individual is a basic, higher or additional rate taxpayer. If the individual is a higher or additional rate taxpayer then CGT is payable at 28%. If the individual is a basic rate taxpayer then CGT is payable at 18% on an amount of taxable gains up to the amount of the taxpayer's unused basic rate band and at 28% on the excess.

HOW IT WORKS

(a) Harold made taxable gains in 2011/12 (ie gains after deduction of the annual exempt amount) of £10,000. Harold is a higher rate taxpayer.

Harold's capital gains tax liability is:

£10,000 × 28%	£2,800

(b) Imelda made taxable gains in 2011/12 (ie gains after deduction of the annual exempt amount) of £32,000. Imelda has taxable income of £25,000.

Imelda has £(35,000 – 25,000) = £10,000 of her basic rate band unused. Imelda's capital gains tax liability is:

	£
£10,000 × 18%	1,800.00
£22,000 × 28%	6,160.00
£32,000	7,960.00

Task 4

Sean made the following chargeable gains and allowable losses in 2011/12.

	£
Gain 12.07.11	21,000
Loss 19.08.11	4,500
Gain 26.02.12	17,500

Sean pays income tax at the additional rate in 2011/12.

The CGT payable for 2011/12 by Sean is:

£	

SELF ASSESSMENT FOR CAPITAL GAINS TAX

A taxpayer who makes capital gain(s) in a tax year is usually required to file details of the gain(s) in a tax return. In many cases, the taxpayer will be filing a tax return for income tax purposes and will include the capital gains supplementary pages.

If, however, the taxpayer only has capital gains to report, he must notify his chargeability to HMRC by 5 October following the end of the tax year. The penalty for late notification is the same as for late notification of income tax chargeability.

The filing date for the tax return is the same as for income tax and the same penalties apply for CGT as for income tax in relation to late filing and errors on the return.

Capital gains tax is payable on 31 January following the end of the tax year. There are no payments on account. The consequences of late payment of CGT are the same as for late payment of income tax so penalties and interest may be charged. Repayment supplement may be paid on overpayments of CGT.

CHATTELS

The rules relating to chattels which we looked at earlier in this Text for companies also apply to disposals by individuals.

CONNECTED PERSONS

If a disposal is made to a connected person the disposal is deemed to take place at the market value of the asset.

If an allowable loss arises on the disposal, it can be set only against gains arising in the same or future years from disposals to the same connected person and the loss can only be set off if he or she is still connected with the person making the loss.

For this purpose an individual is connected with:

- His relatives (brothers, sisters, lineal ancestors and lineal descendants)
- The relatives of his spouse/civil partner
- The spouses/civil partners of his and his spouse's/civil partner's relatives

Task 5

On 1 August 2011 Holly sold a painting to her sister, Emily for £40,000. The market value of the painting on the date of sale was £50,000. Holly had bought the painting for £60,000.

What allowable loss arises on disposal of the painting and how may this be relieved? £10,000 RELIEVED ONLY AGAINST GAINS ON DISPOSALS MADE TO SISTER EMILY

SPOUSES/CIVIL PARTNERS

Spouses/civil partners are taxed as two separate people. Each individual has an annual exempt amount, and losses of one individual cannot be set against gains of the other.

Disposals between spouses/civil partners do not give rise to chargeable gains or allowable losses. The disposal is said to be on a 'NO GAIN/NO LOSS' basis. The acquiring spouse/civil partner takes the base cost of the disposing spouse/civil partner.

Task 6

William sold an asset to his wife Kate in May 2011 for £32,000 when its market value was £45,000. William acquired the asset for £14,000 in June 2001.
What is the chargeable gain on this transfer:

A nil
B £18,000
C £31,000
D £13,000

CHAPTER OVERVIEW

- Chargeable gains are computed for individuals in a similar way to those for companies but there is no indexation allowance
- Taxable gains are net chargeable gains for a tax year minus losses brought forward minus the annual exempt amount
- Losses brought forward can only reduce net chargeable gains down to the annual exempt amount
- CGT is payable at 18% or 28% depending on the individual's taxable income
- The chattels rules apply to disposals by individuals in the same way as for companies
- A disposal to a connected person takes place at market value
- For individuals, connected people are broadly brothers, sisters, lineal ancestors and descendants and their spouses/civil partners plus similar relations of a spouse/civil partner
- Losses on disposals to connected people can only be set against gains on disposals to the same connected person
- Disposals between spouses/civil partners take place on a no gain/no loss basis

Keywords

Taxable gains – the net chargeable gains of a tax year, after deducting losses brought forward and the annual exempt amount

No gain/no loss disposal – a disposal on which no gain or loss arises

TEST YOUR LEARNING

Test 1

Yvette buys an investment property for £325,000. She sells the property on 12 December 2011 for £560,000. Her gain on sale is:

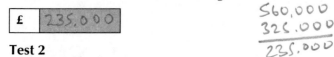

Test 2

Richard sells four acres of land (out of a plot of ten acres) for £38,000 in July 2011. Costs of disposal amount to £3,000. The ten-acre plot cost £41,500. The market value of the six acres remaining is £48,000.

The chargeable gain/allowable loss arising is:

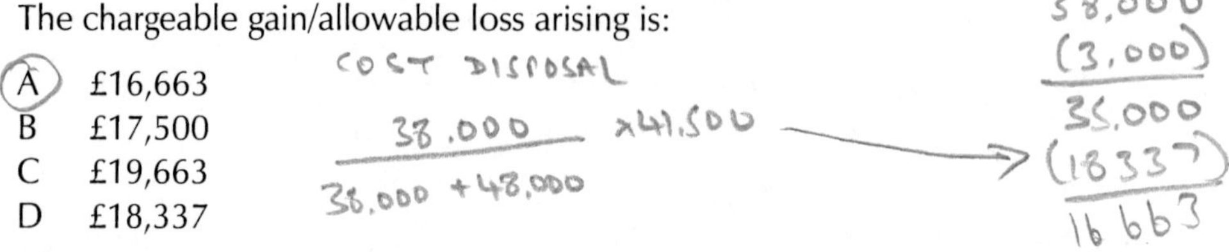

A £16,663
B £17,500
C £19,663
D £18,337

Test 3

Philip has chargeable gains of £171,000 and allowable losses of £5,300 in 2011/12. Losses brought forward at 6 April 2011 are £10,000.

What are the taxable gains for 2011/12?

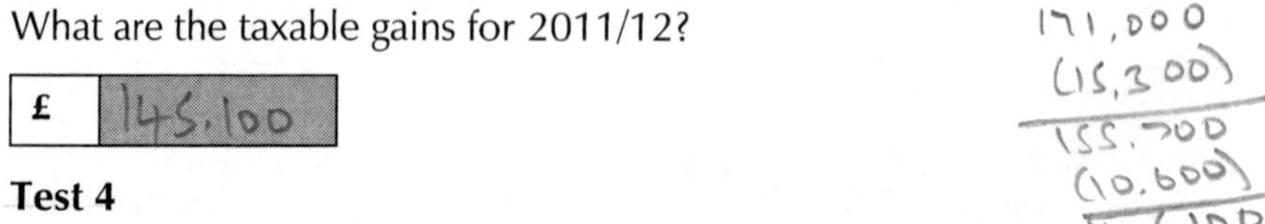

Test 4

Martha's CGT liability for 2011/12, assuming she is a higher rate taxpayer and in August 2011 realised chargeable gains (before the annual exempt amount) of £23,800 is:

Test 5

The payment date for capital gains tax for 2011/12 is:

Test 6

Mustafa bought a non-wasting chattel for £3,500. Compute the gain arising if he sells it for:

(a) £5,800 after deducting selling expenses of £180
(b) £8,200 after deducting selling expenses of £220

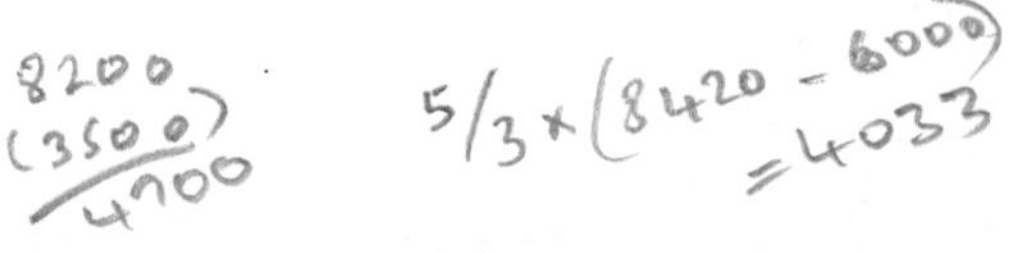

Test 7

Simon bought a racehorse for £4,500. He sold the racehorse for £9,000. The gain arising is:

Test 8

Santa bought a painting for £7,000. He sold the painting in September 2011 for £5,000. The loss arising is:

£

Test 9

True/False. A loss arising on a disposal to a connected person can be set against any gains arising in the same year or in subsequent years.

Test 10

True/False. No gain or loss arises on a disposal to a spouse/civil partner.

Test 11

Indicate with a tick the proceeds that will be used for the following disposals:

	Actual proceeds used	Deemed proceeds (market value) used	No gain or loss basis
Paul sells an asset to his civil partner Joe for £3,600			✓
Grandmother gives an asset to grandchild worth £1,000		✓	
Sarah sells an asset to best friend Cathy for £12,000 worth £20,000		✓	

chapter 16: SHARE DISPOSAL BY INDIVIDUALS

chapter coverage 🕮

In this chapter we see how to compute chargeable gains and allowable losses on the disposal of shares by individuals

The topics covered are:

- Matching rules
- Share pool
- Bonus and rights issues

MATCHING RULES

For individuals the matching of the shares sold is in the following order:

(a) Shares acquired on the same day

(b) Shares acquired in the following thirty days on a FIFO (first in, first out) basis

(c) Shares from the share pool

SHARE POOL

The share pool includes shares acquired up to the day before the disposal on which we are calculating the gain or loss. It grows when an acquisition is made and shrinks when a disposal is made.

The calculation of the share pool value

To compute the value of the share pool, set-up two columns of figures:

(a) The number of shares
(b) The cost of the shares

Each time shares are acquired, both the number and the cost of the acquired shares are added to those already in the pool.

When there is a disposal from the pool, both the number of shares being disposed of, and a cost relating to them, are deducted from the pool. The cost of the disposal is calculated as a proportion of the total cost in the pool, based on the number of shares being sold.

HOW IT WORKS

Jackie bought 10,000 shares in X plc for £6,000 in August 1993 and another 10,000 shares for £9,000 in December 2005.

She sold 12,000 shares for £24,000 in August 2011.

The share pool is:

	No of shares	**Cost**
		£
8.93 Acquisition	10,000	6,000
12.05 Acquisition	10,000	9,000
	20,000	15,000
8.11 Disposal (£15,000 x 12,000/20,000 = £9,000)	(12,000)	(9,000)
c/f	8,000	6,000

The gain is:

	£
Proceeds of sale	24,000
Less: allowable cost	(9,000)
Chargeable gain	15,000

Task 1

Joraver bought 9,000 shares in Z plc for £4,500 in May 1997. He sold 2,000 shares in August 2006. He then bought a further 5,000 shares for £7,500 in May 2009.

Joraver sold 10,000 shares for £20,000 in January 2012.

The gain on the sale in January 2011 is:

£	

HOW IT WORKS

Tony bought shares in A Ltd as follows.

11 May 2002	10,000 shares for £20,000
9 April 2007	5,000 shares for £12,000
15 June 2011	5,000 shares for £15,000

He sold 18,000 shares for £49,500 on 5 June 2011.

The disposal is matched first against the acquisition in the next 30 days as follows.

	£
Proceeds of sale $\frac{5,000}{18,000} \times £49,500$	13,750
Less: allowable cost	(15,000)
Allowable loss	(1,250)

Then the disposal is matched against the share pool.

	£
Proceeds of sale $\frac{13,000}{18,000} \times £49,500$	35,750
Less: allowable cost (W)	(27,733)
Chargeable gain	8,017

Therefore the net chargeable gain is:

£(8,017 – 1,250)	6,767

Working	**No of shares**	**Cost**
		£
11.5.02 Acquisition	10,000	20,000
9.4.07 Acquisition	5,000	12,000
	15,000	32,000
5.6.11 Disposal	(13,000)	(27,733)
c/f	2,000	4,267

Task 2

Eliot acquired shares in K Ltd as follows.

10 August 2004	5,000 shares for £10,000
15 April 2007	2,000 shares for £5,000
25 July 2011	1,000 shares for £3,800
27 July 2011	500 shares for £1,700

Eliot sold 6,000 shares for £21,600 on 25 July 2011.

Calculate the net chargeable gain arising on the disposal by Eliot.

BONUS AND RIGHTS ISSUES

Bonus issues

BONUS ISSUE SHARES are additional shares given free to shareholders based on their current holding(s). For example, a shareholder may own 2,000 shares. The company makes a 1 share for every 2 shares held bonus issue (called 1 for 2 bonus issue). The shareholder will then have an extra 1,000 shares, giving him 3,000 shares overall.

Bonus shares are treated as being acquired at the date of the original acquisition of the underlying shares giving rise to the bonus issue.

Since bonus shares are issued at no cost there is no need to adjust the original cost.

Rights issues

In a RIGHTS ISSUE, a shareholder is offered additional shares by the company in proportion to the shares he already holds.

The difference between a bonus issue and a rights issue is that in a rights issue the new shares are paid for. This results in an adjustment to the original cost.

HOW IT WORKS

Jonah acquired 20,000 shares for £36,000 in T plc in April 2002. There was a 1 for 2 bonus issue in May 2007 and a 1 for 5 rights issue in August 2011 at £1.20 per share.

Jonah sold 30,000 shares for £45,000 in December 2011.

The share pool is constructed as follows:

	No of shares	Cost
		£
4.02 Acquisition	20,000	36,000
5.07 Bonus 1 for 2	10,000	–
	30,000	36,000
8.11 Rights 1 for 5 @ £1.20	6,000	7,200
	36,000	43,200
12.11 Disposal	(30,000)	(36,000)
c/f	6,000	7,200

The gain on sale is:

	£
Proceeds of sale	45,000
Less: allowable cost	(36,000)
Chargeable gain	9,000

Task 3

Dorothy bought 2,000 shares for £10,000 in S Ltd in August 2002. There was a 1 for 1 rights issue at £2.50 in May 2005 and Dorothy took up all her rights issue shares. There was a 1 for 4 bonus issue in September 2008.

Dorothy sold 3,000 shares for £18,000 in October 2011.

Her chargeable gain on sale is:

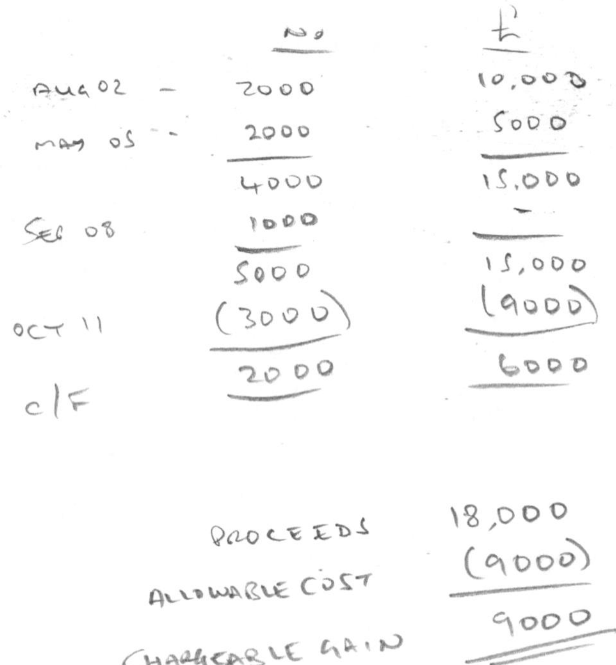

No
£
AUG 02 - 2000 10,000
MAY 05 - 2000 5000
4000 15,000
SEP 08 1000 -
5000 15,000
OCT 11 (3000) (9000)
2000 6000
c/F
PROCEEDS 18,000
ALLOWABLE COST (9000)
CHARGEABLE GAIN 9000

CHAPTER OVERVIEW

- The matching rules for individuals are:
  - Same day acquisitions
  - Next 30 days acquisitions on a FIFO basis
  - Shares in the share pool
- The share pool runs up to the day before disposal
- Bonus issue and rights issue shares are acquired in proportion to the shareholder's existing holding
- The difference between a bonus and a rights issue is that in a rights issue shares are paid for

Keywords

Bonus issue shares – shares that are issued free to shareholders based on original holdings

Rights issues – similar to bonus issues except that in a rights issue shares must be paid for

TEST YOUR LEARNING

Test 1

Tasha bought 10,000 shares in V plc in August 1992 for £5,000 and a further 10,000 shares for £16,000 in April 2007. She sold 15,000 shares for £30,000 in November 2011.

Her chargeable gain is:

A £9,000
B £11,500
C £17,000
D £14,250

Test 2

True/False: in both a bonus issue and a rights issue, there is an adjustment to the original cost of the shares.

Test 3

Marcus bought 2,000 shares in X plc in May 2001 for £12,000. There was a 1 for 2 rights issue at £7.50 per share in December 2002. Marcus sold 2,500 shares for £20,000 in March 2012. His chargeable gain is:

£	

chapter 17: RELIEFS FOR CHARGEABLE GAINS

chapter coverage 🕮

In this chapter we consider three reliefs for chargeable gains.

Entrepreneurs' relief reduces the effective rate of CGT on the disposal of certain business assets to 10%.

The basic principle of the other two reliefs is that a gain is deferred by deducting it from a base cost to be used to calculate a future gain. This lower base cost causes a larger gain to arise in the future. The deferred gain is often said to be 'held-over' or 'rolled-over'.

The topics that we shall cover are:

- Entrepreneurs' relief
- Replacement of business assets/rollover relief
- Gift relief

ENTREPRENEURS' RELIEF

Introduction

Individuals can claim ENTREPRENEURS' RELIEF to reduce the rate of CGT on a material disposal of business assets. Gains on assets qualifying for entrepreneurs relief are taxed at 10% regardless of the level of a person's taxable income.

Lifetime limit

There is a lifetime limit is £10 million of gains on which entrepreneurs' relief can be claimed.

HOW IT WORKS

Carrie has made several disposals qualifying for entrepreneurs' relief. The gains on these disposals are as follows:

1 May 2011	£7,750,000
1 June 2011	£2,300,000
1 February 2012	£2,200,000

Entrepreneurs' relief will be given on the following amounts:

1 May 2011 £7,750,000 (less than the lifetime limit of £10,000,000)

1 June 2011 £2,250,000 (lifetime limit £10,000,000 less relief already used of £7,750,000). £50,000 is not eligible for relief

1 February 2012 None of the lifetime limit left therefore £2,200,000 is not eligible for entrepreneurs' relief.

Conditions for entrepreneurs' relief

Entrepreneurs' relief is available where there is a material disposal of business assets.

A material disposal of business assets is:

(a) A disposal of the whole or part of a business that has been owned by the individual throughout the period of one year ending with the date of the disposal

(b) A disposal of one or more assets in use for the purposes of a business at the time at which the business ceases to be carried on provided that:

   (i) The business was owned by the individual throughout the period of one year ending with the date on which the business ceases to be carried on; and

   (ii) The date of cessation is within three years ending with the date of the disposal.

(c) A disposal of shares or securities of a company where the company is the individual's personal company; the company is a trading company; the individual is an officer (eg a director) or employee of the company and these conditions are met either:

   (i) Throughout the period of one year ending with the date of the disposal; or

   (ii) Throughout the period of one year ending with the date on which the company ceases to be a trading company and that date is within the period of three years ending with the date of the disposal

For condition (a) to apply, there has to be a disposal of the whole or part of the business as a going concern, not just a disposal of individual assets. A business includes one carried on as a partnership of which the individual is a partner. The business must be a trade, profession or vocation conducted on a commercial basis with a view to the realisation of profits.

For both conditions (a) and (b), relief is only available on relevant business assets. These are assets used for the purposes of the business and cannot include shares and securities or assets held as investments.

For condition (c), a personal company in relation to an individual is one where:

(a) the individual holds at least 5% of the ordinary share capital; and

(b) the individual can exercise at least 5% of the voting rights in the company by virtue of that holding of shares.

Task 1

The following assets are disposed of in 2011/12 by various individuals. Which, if any, are qualifying disposals for entrepreneurs' relief?

(a) Part of a business in which the individual has been a partner since August 2009

(b) A freehold factory which the individual uses in his business and has owned for 10 years

(c) Unquoted shares held by the individual in a personal trading company in which he is employed and has owned for the previous two years

(d) Quoted shares held by the individual in a personal trading company in which he is employed and has owned for the previous two years

Operation of the relief

Where there is a material disposal of business assets that results in both gains and losses, losses are set off against gains to give a single gain on the disposal of the business assets.

The rate of tax on this chargeable gain is 10%.

HOW IT WORKS

Sally sells her business in August 2011, realising the following gains and losses:

	£
Goodwill	120,000
Machine	122,000
Workshop	(42,000)

All the assets qualify for entrepreneurs' relief and she has no other chargeable disposals in the year.

The CGT payable on the disposal is:

	£
Net gains	200,000
Less: annual exempt amount	(10,600)
Taxable gains	189,400
CGT @ 10%	18,940.00

In order to use losses and the annual exempt amount in the most beneficial manner, they should be set against gains that do not qualify for entrepreneurs' relief in order to save tax at either 18% or 28%.

HOW IT WORKS

Robbie started in business as a manufacturer of widgets in July 2001. He acquired a freehold workshop for £86,000 in May 2003. He used the workshop in his business. In August 2007, Robbie invested £40,000 of his business profits in shares in an investment company. He bought a machine for use in his business in January 2011 at a cost of £35,000.

In November 2011, Robbie sold his business to a larger competitor. The sale proceeds were apportioned to capital assets as follows.

	£
Goodwill	50,000
Workshop	125,000
Shares	80,500
Machine	38,000

Robbie also had a loss brought forward of £1,000, but made no other disposals in 2011/12. He is a higher rate taxpayer.

Robbie's CGT liability on the disposal is calculated as follows:

	£	£
Proceeds of goodwill	50,000	
Less: cost	(nil)	50,000
Proceeds of workshop	125,000	
Less: cost	(86,000)	39,000
Proceeds of machine (N1)	38,000	
Less: cost	(35,000)	3,000
Gains qualifying for entrepreneur's relief		92,000
Proceeds of shares (N2)	80,500	
Less: cost	(40,000)	40,500
Chargeable gains		132,500
Less: loss b/fwd		(1,000)
Less: annual exempt amount		(10,600)
Taxable gains		120,900
CGT payable		
£92,000 x 10% (gains eligible for entrepreneurs' relief)		9,200.00
£28,900 x 28% (other gains) (N3)		8,092.00
		17,292.00

Notes

1. The gain on the machine is eligible for entrepreneurs' relief even though it has not been owned for one year. The condition is that the individual has owned the business for one year.
2. The gain on the shares is not eligible for entrepreneurs' relief because the shares are not relevant business assets.
3. The loss brought forward and the annual exempt amount are set against the gains not eligible for entrepreneurs' relief.

Unused basic rate band

Earlier chapter in this Text, we established that if an individual is a basic rate taxpayer then CGT is payable at 18% on taxable gains up to the amount of the taxpayer's unused basic rate band and at 28% on the excess.

Although chargeable gains that qualify for entrepreneurs' relief are always taxed at a rate of 10%, they must be taken into account when establishing the rate to apply to other capital gains. Chargeable gains qualifying for entrepreneurs' relief therefore reduce the amount of any unused basic rate band.

HOW IT WORKS

(a) Steve sells his business, all the assets of which qualify for entrepreneurs' relief, in August 2011. The gains arising are £15,000. He also sold investments in November 2011 realising chargeable gains of £40,000. £10,000 of Steve's basic rate band was unused.

The CGT payable is:

	£
Gains eligible for entrepreneurs' relief	15,000
Other gains	40,000
Chargeable gains	55,000
Less: annual exempt amount (set against other gains)	(10,600)
Taxable gains	44,400

CGT payable	
£15,000 x 10% (gains eligible for entrepreneurs' relief)	1,500.00
£29,400 x 28% (other gains less annual exempt amount)	8,232.00
	9,732.00

The taxable gains eligible for entrepreneurs' relief exceeded Steve's unused basic rate band so the other gains, after the deduction of the annual exempt amount, are taxable at 28%.

(b) Steve sells his business, all the assets of which qualify for entrepreneurs' relief, in August 2011. The gains arising are £15,000. He also sold investments in November 2011 realising chargeable gains of £40,000. £20,000 of Steve's basic rate band was unused.

The CGT payable is:

	£
Gains eligible for entrepreneurs' relief	15,000
Other gains	40,000
Chargeable gains	55,000
Less: annual exempt amount (set against other gains)	(10,600)
Taxable gains	44,400

CGT payable	
£15,000 × 10% (gains eligible for entrepreneurs' relief)	1,500.00
£5,000 × 18% (£20,000 - £15,000 of Steve's basic rate band is unused)	900.00
£24,400 x 28% (balance of other gains)	6,832.00
	9,232.00

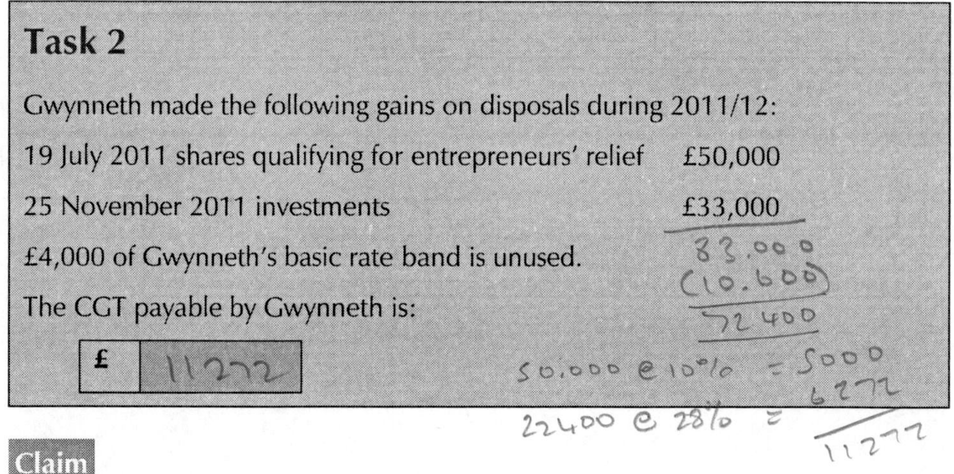

Task 2

Gwynneth made the following gains on disposals during 2011/12:

19 July 2011 shares qualifying for entrepreneurs' relief	£50,000
25 November 2011 investments	£33,000

£4,000 of Gwynneth's basic rate band is unused.

The CGT payable by Gwynneth is:

£ ______

Claim

An individual must claim entrepreneurs' relief. The claim deadline is the first anniversary of 31 January following the end of the tax year of disposal. For a 2011/12 disposal, the taxpayer must claim by 31 January 2014.

Task 3

Lewis bought 10,000 ordinary shares in V Ltd in May 2002 for £50,000 which was a 10% holding. V Ltd is a trading company and Lewis was appointed as a director of the company in June 2004. He bought a further 1,000 shares for £10,000 in August 2009.

Lewis sold 2,200 of his shares in July 2011 for £33,500.

During 2011/12 he also realised a gain on the sale of a painting of £17,000, and had losses brought forward of £1,300. He has £3,400 of his basic rate band remaining unused.

USED UP BY ENTREPRENEURS

(1) Using the pro forma layout provided, show the share pool of shares in V Ltd owned by Lewis.

	No of shares	*Cost*
		£
MAY 02 ACQUISITION	10000	50,000
AUG 09 "	1000	10,000
	11,000	60,000
JUL 11 DISPOSAL	(2200)	(12,000)
C/F	8800	48,000

(2) Using the pro forma layout provided, calculate the CGT payable for 2011/12.

	£
SHARES:	
PROCEEDS OF SALE	33,500
LESS ALLOWABLE COST	12,000
ELIGIBLE FOR ENTREPRENEURS' RELIEF	21,500
PAINTING (NOT ELIGIBLE)	17,000
LOSS B/F	(1300)
ANNUAL EXEMPT AMOUNT	(10,600)
TAXABLE GAIN	26,600
SHARES 21,500 @ 10%	2150
PAINTING 5100 @ 28%	1428

REPLACEMENT OF BUSINESS ASSETS/ROLLOVER RELIEF

A gain may be 'rolled-over' where it arises on the disposal of a business asset (the 'old' asset) if another business asset (the 'new' asset) is acquired.

The following conditions must be met.

- The old asset and the new asset must be used in a trade
- The old asset and the new asset must both be qualifying assets. Qualifying assets include:
  - Land and buildings used for the purpose of the trade
  - Fixed (that is, immoveable) plant and machinery
  - Goodwill (for individuals only)
- Reinvestment of the proceeds of the old asset must take place in a period beginning one year before and ending three years after the date of the disposal.
- For all the gain to be deferred all the proceeds of the old asset must be reinvested in the new asset

The new asset can be for use in a different trade from the old asset. Deferral is obtained by deducting the gain on the old asset from the cost of the new asset.

ROLLOVER RELIEF is available to both individuals and companies.

HOW IT WORKS

A freehold factory was purchased by a sole trader on 13 May 1999 for £60,000 and sold for £90,000 on 18 September 2011. A replacement factory was purchased on 6 December 2011 for £100,000. Rollover relief was claimed on the sale of the first factory.

(a) *Gain on sale September 2011*

	£
Disposal proceeds	90,000
Less: cost	(60,000)
Gain (to defer)	30,000

(b) *Revised base cost of asset purchased in December 2011*

	£
Original cost	100,000
Less: rolled over gain	(30,000)
Revised base cost	70,000

Task 4

George bought a freehold factory for business use in August 2007 for £35,000. It was sold in March 2012 for £90,000. A replacement factory was purchased in April 2011 for £120,000 and rollover relief was claimed.

(1) The gain on the sale of the factory in March 2012 is:

(2) The gain that can be rolled over is:

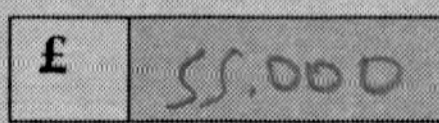

(3) The base cost of the new factory acquired in April 2011 is:

Task 5

Louis bought office premises for £80,000 in July 2007. He sold them for £100,000 in May 2011. Louis bought a freehold factory for use in his business in June 2011 at a cost of £350,000 and claimed rollover relief in respect of the gain on the office premises. Louis sold the factory for £375,000 in September 2013.

(1) The gain on the sale of the office premises in May 2011 is:

(2) The gain rolled over into the factory is:

(3) The gain on the sale of the factory is:

Sale proceeds not fully reinvested

If the proceeds of the sale of an asset are not fully reinvested in a new qualifying asset, an amount of the gain equal to the proceeds not reinvested is immediately chargeable. The balance of the gain can be rolled over.

HOW IT WORKS

Susannah realised a gain of £300,000 on the disposal of an office block used in her business. The office block was sold for £700,000. A new office block factory was bought for £600,000 in the following month.

The proceeds not reinvested are £100,000 so this amount of the gain is immediately chargeable. £200,000 of the gain can be rolled over and set against the base cost of the new office block. This means the base cost of the new office block is £(600,000 – 200,000) = £400,000.

Task 6

A sole trader sold a factory in July 2011 for £670,000 realising a gain of £120,000. In September 2011 a replacement factory was bought for £650,000. Advise the sole trader as to whether a chargeable gain will arise on the sale of the first factory. Assume rollover relief is claimed where possible.

HOW IT WORKS

D Ltd acquired a factory in April 2006 at a cost of £120,000. It used the factory in its trade throughout the period of its ownership.

In August 2011, D Ltd sold the factory for £210,000. In November 2011, it acquired another factory at a cost of £180,000.

The indexed rise between April 2006 and August 2011 is 0.177.

The gain on sale is:

	£
Proceeds	210,000
Less: cost	(120,000)
	90,000
Less: indexation allowance 0.177 × £120,000	(21,240)
	68,760
Less: rollover relief (balancing figure)	(38,760)
Chargeable gain: amount not reinvested	
£(210,000 - 180,000)	30,000

The base cost of the new factory is:

	£
Cost of second factory	180,000
Less: rolled over gain	(38,760)
Base cost	141,240

Task 7

H Ltd acquired a warehouse in May 2005 for £75,000. It used the warehouse in its trade throughout the period of its ownership.

H Ltd sold the warehouse for £120,000 in August 2011. It had acquired a workshop for £100,000 in March 2011.

The indexed rise between May 2005 and August 2011 is 0.209.

(1) The gain on sale of the warehouse in August 2011 assuming that rollover relief is claimed is:

£	

(2) The base cost of the workshop is:

£	

GIFT RELIEF

Individuals can claim GIFT RELIEF to defer a gain otherwise arising on the gift of a business asset. The gift is deemed to be made at market value.

The transferee is deemed to acquire the asset for its market value less the deferred gain.

HOW IT WORKS

John bought a business asset in 2007 for £20,000. On 1 May 2011 John gave the asset to Marie Louise. The market value of the asset on the date of the gift was £90,000.

John is deemed to dispose of the asset for its market value of £90,000 so the gain arising on the gift is:

	£
Deemed disposal proceeds	90,000
Less: cost	(20,000)
Gain	70,000

The gain of £70,000 is deferred by setting it against the value of £90,000 at which Marie Louise is deemed to acquire the gift. Therefore Marie Louise is deemed to acquire the gift for £20,000 and this will be used as the base cost for future disposals.

Task 8

Archie purchased business premises in July 2003 for £80,000. In December 2007 Archie gave the premises, then valued at £400,000, to Hugo and claimed gift relief. Hugo continued to run a business from the premises but decided to sell them in May 2011 for £675,000.

(1) The gift relief on the gift made in December 2007 is:

£	320,000

(2) The gain on the sale in May 2011 is:

£	595,000

Qualifying assets for gift relief purposes include:

(a) Assets used in a trade carried on:

- (i) by the donor, or
- (ii) by the donor's personal company

(b) Shares in:

- (i) an unquoted trading company or
- (ii) the donor's personal trading company.

A 'personal company' is one in which not less than 5% of the voting rights are controlled by the donor.

Task 9

Deidre gives the following assets to Steve. Which, if any, are qualifying assets for the purposes of gift relief?

An antique painting

Quoted shares in a trading company of which Deidre controls 1%.

Unquoted trading company shares.

A freehold factory that Deidre has always used in her printing business.

Task 10

Julie bought 10,000 shares in an unquoted trading company for £50,000 in July 2003. Julie gave her shares to Jack in May 2011 when they were worth £85,000. Jack sold the shares for £95,000 in December 2012.

Neither Julie nor Jack had made any other disposals in 2011/12 or 2012/13.

(1) If gift relief is not claimed, Julie's chargeable gain is:

£	

and Jack's chargeable gain is:

£	

(2) If gift relief is claimed, Julie's chargeable gain is:

£	

and Jack's chargeable gain is:

£	

CHAPTER OVERVIEW

- Entrepreneurs' relief reduces the rate of CGT on gains made by an individual on certain business disposals to 10%
- There is a lifetime limit of £10 million for entrepreneurs' relief
- Entrepreneurs' relief applies to disposals of an unincorporated business (or part of a business), disposals of business assets on cessation, and shares in a trading company that is the individual's personal company and of which he is an officer or employee
- Rollover relief can be used by individuals and companies to defer a gain when a qualifying business asset is replaced with another qualifying business asset
- Qualifying business assets for rollover relief include land and buildings, fixed plant and machinery and, for individuals, goodwill. Both the old and the new assets must be used for the purposes of a trade
- If sale proceeds are not fully reinvested an amount of the gain equal to the proceeds not reinvested is immediately chargeable. The remainder of the gain may be rolled over
- The rolled over gain reduces the cost of the new asset
- The new asset must be acquired in the period commencing one year before and ending three years after the disposal
- Gift relief can be used by an individual to defer a gain on the gift of business assets
- The transferee acquires the gift at its market value less the amount of the deferred gain
- Qualifying assets for gift relief include assets used in a trade by the donor or his personal company, unquoted shares in a trading company and shares in a personal trading company

Keywords

Entrepreneurs' relief – Reduces the effective rate of tax on the disposal of certain business assets from 18% or 28% to 10%

Rollover relief – Can defer a gain when business assets are replaced

Gift relief – Can defer a gain on a gift of business assets by an individual

TEST YOUR LEARNING

Test 1

Ian sold his business as a going concern to John in May 2011. The gains on sale were £10,400,000. Ian had not previously made any claims for entrepreneurs' relief, and made no other disposals in 2011/12. Ian is a higher rate taxpayer. Ian's CGT liability for 2011/12 is:

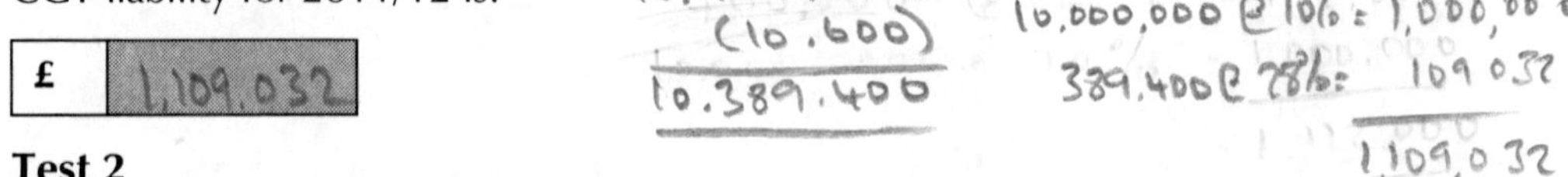

£	

Test 2

Jemma sold her shareholding in J Ltd in January 2012. She had acquired the shares in August 2002 for £10,000. The proceeds of sale were £80,000. The disposal qualified for entrepreneurs' relief. Jemma's CGT on the disposal, assuming she has already used the annual exempt amount for 2011/12, is:

£	

Test 3

K Ltd sold a factory on 10 November 2011. It purchased the following assets:

Date of purchase	*Asset*
21 September 2010	Office block
15 February 2012	Freehold Factory
4 June 2013	Fork lift truck
8 December 2014	Freehold warehouse

All of the above assets are used for the purpose of the trade of K Ltd.

Against which purchase may K Ltd claim rollover relief in respect of the gain arising on disposal of the factory?

A Office block
B Factory
C Fork lift truck
D Warehouse

Test 4

Trevor bought land for £100,000 in March 2004. In March 2011, this land was sold for £400,000 and replacement land was bought for £380,000. The replacement land was sold in May 2012 for £500,000. Both pieces of land were used in Trevor's trade, which is still continuing.

What is the chargeable gain arising in May 2012? Assume all available reliefs were claimed.

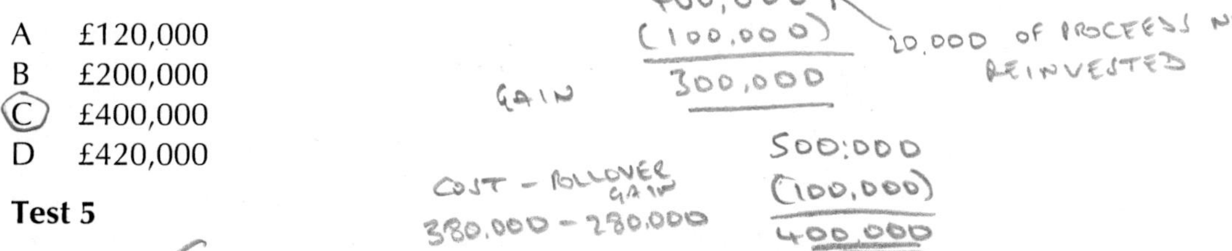

A £120,000
B £200,000
C £400,000
D £420,000

Test 5

True or false: provided both assets are used in Mr Astro's trade, a gain arising on the sale of freehold land and buildings can be rolled over against the cost of goodwill.

Test 6

Freehold land and buildings are sold on 15 January 2012.

If relief for replacement of business assets is to be claimed, a new asset must be acquired between

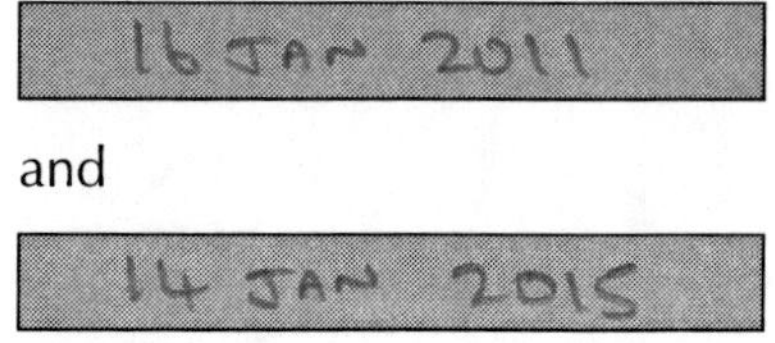

and

Test 7

H Ltd sells a warehouse for £400,000. The warehouse cost £220,000 and the indexation allowance available is £40,000. The company acquires another warehouse ten months later for £375,000 and claims rollover relief.

The chargeable gain after rollover relief is:

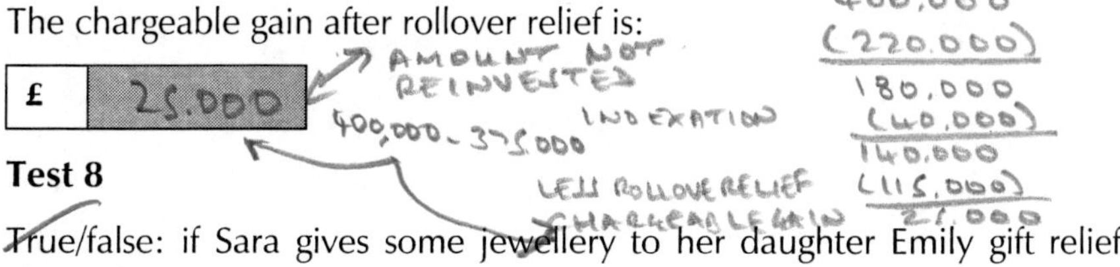

£

Test 8

True/false: if Sara gives some jewellery to her daughter Emily gift relief can be claimed.

Test 9

Tommy gave Sinbad a factory in June 2011 that had been used in his trade. The factory cost £50,000 in October 2003 and was worth £200,000 at the date of the gift. Sinbad sold the factory for £350,000 in May 2012.

If gift relief is claimed, the gain on the gift by Tommy is:

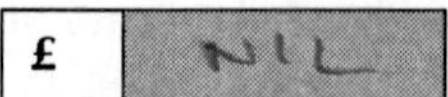

and the gain on the sale by Sinbad is:

ANSWERS TO CHAPTER TASKS

Chapter 1: The tax framework

1

	Non-savings income	**Savings income**	**Dividend income**	**Total**
	£	**£**	**£**	**£**
Trading income	16,000			
Building society interest		6,000		
Dividends			8,750	
Net income	16,000	6,000	8,750	30,750
Less: personal allowance	(7,475)			(7,475)
Taxable income	8,525	6,000	8,750	23,275

2

	£
£35,000 × 20%	7,000.00
£15,000 × 40%	6,000.00
£50,000	13,000.00

3

	£
Non-savings income	
£1,500 × 20%	300.00
Savings income	
£1,060 × 10%	106.00
£28,940 × 20%	5,788.00
£30,000	
Dividend income	
£3,500 × 10%	350.00
£5,000 × 32.5%	1,625.00
£8,500	8,169.00

4

	£
Non-savings income	
£35,000 × 20%	7,000.00
£85,000 × 40%	34,000.00
£120,000	
Dividend income	
£30,000 × 32.5%	9,750.00
£25,000 × 42.5%	10,625.00
£55,000	61,375.00

Chapter 2: Capital allowances

1

	Revenue	Capital
Rent paid on premises	✓	
Purchase of machinery		✓
Repairs to machinery	✓	
Redecoration of premises	✓	

2 (1) The AIA can be claimed on:

	Claim	Not claim
Computer	✓	
General lighting in showroom		✓
Office furniture	✓	
Digger	✓	

(2) Since the eligible expenditure of £104,000 exceeds the maximum amount of the AIA, the maximum claim that can be made is **£100,000**.

3

	Main pool	Allowances
	£	£
B/f	10,000	
Addition (no AIA on car)	8,000	
Disposal	(6,000)	
	12,000	
WDA @ 20%	(2,400)	2,400
C/f	9,600	

4

	AIA	Main pool	Allowances
	£	£	£
Y/e 31 December 2011			
B/f		10,000	
AIA additions			
10.7.11 Machine	73,000		
15.11.11 Lorry	47,000		
	120,000		
AIA	(100,000)		100,000
	20,000		
Transfer balance to main pool	(20,000)	20,000	
		30,000	
WDA@ 20%		(6,000)	6,000
C/f		24,000	
Capital allowances			106,000

5

	Main pool	Allowance
	£	£
B/f	47,000	
Less: disposal (restricted to cost)	(7,000)	
	40,000	
WDA @ 20%	(8,000)	8,000
C/f	32,000	

6

	Main pool	Allowance
	£	£
B/f	20,000	
Non AIA addition	4,000	
	24,000	
WDA @ 20% × 3/12	(1,200)	1,200
C/f	22,800	

7

	AIA	Main pool	Allowances
	£	£	£
P/e 31 December 2011			
B/f		12,000	
AIA additions			
14.6.11 Furniture	20,000		
15.8.11 Machinery	55,000		
	75,000		
AIA £100,000 × 8/12	(66,667)		66,667
	8,333		
Transfer to main pool	(8,333)	8,333	
		20,333	
WDA@ 20% × 8/12		(2,711)	2,711
C/f		17,622	
Capital allowances			69,378

The AIA and WDA are prorated in the short period.

8

	Special rate pool	Allowances
	£	£
10 months ended 5 April 2012		
Addition	18,000	
WDA £18,000 @ 10% × 10/12	(1,500)	1,500
C/f	16,500	

9 *Year ended 5 April 2012*

	Private use asset		Allowances 75%
	£		£
Car	20,000		
WDA £20,000 @ 10%	(2,000)	× 75%	1,500
C/f	18,000		

10

	Nissan 75% business use		Ford	Allowances
	£		£	£
y/e 5 April 2012				
B/f	19,000		9,600	
WDA @ lower of £19,000 @ 20%				
and £3,000	(3,000)	× 75%		2,250
WDA @ 20%			(1,920)	1,920
C/f	16,000		7,680	
Capital allowances				4,170

Private use by the employee is not relevant to Leonora's capital allowances claim. The employee will be taxed on a benefit of employment for this private use (this topic is covered in Personal Tax).

The Ford is dealt with in its own pool because it was an expensive car when it was bought. This treatment applies for the whole of the ownership of the car by Leonora even after the brought forward value of the car falls below £12,000.

Chapter 3: Computing trading income

1

	Revenue	**Capital**
Paying employee wages	✓	
Paying rent for premises	✓	
Buying machinery		✓
Buying a van		✓
Building an extension to shop		✓
Paying for repairs to car	✓	

2 False

As the cinema was usable on acquisition the repair expenditure is allowable. This point was decided in the case of *Odeon Associated Theatres v Jones*. You do not need to remember case names for assessment purposes.

3

	£
Net profit in accounts	38,000
Add: entertaining expenses	2,000
depreciation	4,000
	44,000
Less: capital allowances	(3,500)
Taxable trading profit	40,500

4 40% × £600 = £240 must be added back in computing taxable profits.

5 £100 must be added back. HMRC allow the deduction of donations to small local charities.

6 **A**

£7,000.

The expenses relating to the employee service contracts are allowable as this is a revenue item.

The expenses relating to the purchase of new offices are disallowable as they relate to a capital item. Legal expenses relating to the renewal of a short lease are specifically allowable.

7 C

£18,450.

The redundancy payments are allowable. The payment of a salary to the proprietor of a business is not deductible because it is just a method of extracting a profit from the business and that profit is taxable in the normal way. 15% of leasing costs of car with CO_2 emissions exceeding 160g/km are disallowable.

8

	£
Heating (70%)	**560**

The private portion of the above bill must be added back in computing taxable trading profits.

9

	£
Entertaining Customers	**7,300**

10

	£	£
Net profit in accounts		12,710
Add: Depreciation	1,500	
Provision against a fall in raw material prices	5,000	
Entertainment expenses	750	
Legal expenses (relate to a capital item)	250	
		7,500
		20,210
Less rental income received (to tax as property income)		(860)
Adjusted trading profit		19,350

Chapter 4: Taxing unincorporated businesses

1 C

1 October 2010 to 30 September 2011.

2

Tax year	Basis period	Taxable profits £
2010/11	1 June 2010 to 5 April 2011	£10,000
2011/12	1 June 2010 to 31 May 2011	£12,000
2012/13	1 June 2011 to 31 May 2012	£21,000

In 2010/11 the taxable profits are £12,000 x 10/12 = £10,000

3

Tax year	Basis period	Taxable profits £
2009/10	1 July 2008 to 30 June 2009	£12,000
2010/11	1 July 2009 to 30 June 2010	£8,000
2011/12	1 July 2010 to 31 January 2012	£11,000

In 2011/12 taxable profits are £6,000 + £5,000 = £11,000

4 (1)

Tax year	Basis period	Taxable profits £
2009/10	1 March 2010 to 5 April 2010	£2,000
2010/11	6 April 2010 to 5 April 2011	£24,000
2011/12	1 July 2010 to 30 June 2011	£24,000
2012/13	1 July 2011 to 30 June 2012	£36,800

In 2009/10, taxable profits are £32,000 × 1/16 = £2,000

In 2010/11, taxable profits are £32,000 × 12/16 = £24,000

In 2011/12, taxable profits are £32,000 × 12/16 = £24,000

(2) Overlap profits

1 July 2010 to 5 April 2011 (£32,000 × 9/16) = £18,000

5

Tax year	**Basis period**	**Taxable profits**
		£
2007/08	1 May 2007 to 5 April 2008	13,750
2008/09	1 May 2007 to 30 April 2008	15,000
2009/10	1 May 2008 to 30 April 2009	9,000
2010/11	1 May 2009 to 30 April 2010	10,500
2011/12	1 May 2010 to 31 January 2012	3,200
Total taxable profits		51,450

In 2007/08 taxable profits are (£15,000 × 11/12) = £13,750

Overlap profits 1 May 2007 to 5 April 2008 (£15,000 × 11/12) = £13,750. This amount is deducted in the final year of trading.

In 2011/12 taxable profits are (£16,000 + £950 – £13,750) = £3,200

Chapter 5: Partnerships

1

	Total	Roger	Muggles
	£	£	£
Salaries	60,000	30,000	30,000
Profit (210,000 – 60,000)	150,000	120,000	30,000
Taxable trading profits	210,000	**150,000**	**60,000**

2

	Total	James	Kieran	Jemima
	£	£	£	£
Interest	3,000	1,000	1,000	1,000
Salary	70,000		35,000	35,000
Profits	197,000	118,200	39,400	39,400
Taxable trading profits	270,000	119,200	75,400	75,400

3

	£
1 July 2010 to 31 March 2011	60,000
1 April 2011 to 30 June 2011	20,000
Total profits	80,000

	Total	Hansel	Greta
	£	£	£
To 31 March 2011	60,000	30,000	30,000
1 April 2011 to 30 June 2011	20,000	16,000	4,000
	80,000	46,000	34,000

4

	Total	New partner (30%)
	£	
Year ended 31 October 2010		
1 November 2009 to 31 May 2010 (7/12)	19,950	–
1 June 2010 to 31 October 2010 (5/12)	14,250	4,275
	34,200	
Year ended 31 October 2011	45,600	13,680

The new partner is taxed using the opening year rules from 2010/11:

2010/11 (1 June 2010 to 5 April 2011)

£4,275 + 5/12 × £13,680 = **£9,975**

Overlap profits are 5/12 × £13,680 = **£5,700**

2011/12 (year ended 31 October 2011) = **£13,680**

5

	Total	**X**	**Y**	**Z**
	£	**£**	**£**	**£**
Year ended 31 March 2010	24,000	8,000	8,000	8,000
Year ended 31 March 2011				
1 April 2010 to 30 June 2010 (3/12)	3,500	1,167	1,167	1,166
1 July 2010 to 31 March 2011(9/12)	10,500		6,300	4,200
	14,000	1,167	7,467	5,366
Year ended 31 March 2012	48,000		28,800	19,200

Y and Z are taxed on a continuing basis of assessment throughout.

	X	**Y**	**Z**
2009/10 (y/e 31 March 2010)	8,000	8,000	8,000
2010/11 (y/e 31 March 2011)	1,167	7,467	5,366
2011/12 (y/e 31 March 2012)	0	28,800	19,200

Chapter 6: Losses

	£
Total income	21,000
Less: loss	(21,000)
Net income	NIL

Loss c/f £30,000 – £21,000 = £9,000

The loss is deducted from total income to compute net income. Since the personal allowance is deducted from net income, the benefit of the personal allowance is wasted.

Chapter 7: National insurance

1

Class 2 NICs	
52 × £2.50	**£130.00**
Class 4 NICs	
9% × (£25,000 – 7,225)	**£1,599.75**

2 **A**

Class 2 NICs	
52 × £2.50	£130.00
Class 4 NICs	
	£
9% × (£42,475- £7,225)	3,172.50
2% × (£60,000 – 42,475)	350.50
	3,523.00
Total NICs £(130.00 + 3,523.00)	**3,653.00**

Chapter 8: Self assessment for individuals

1 Since the notice to file was issued after 31 October 2012, the filing date is three months after the notice was issued, ie **2 February 2013**.

2 Kelly's penalty can be reduced from **70%** of the potential lost revenue (for a deliberate, but not concealed error) to **20%**, with the unprompted disclosure of her error.

3 Payments on account for 2012/13 $\frac{£14,000}{2}$ = £7,000 each due on 31 January 2013 and 31 July 2013.

Chapter 9: Computing taxable total profits

1 (1) *Capital allowances*

	Main pool	Allowances
	£	£
B/f	21,500	
Addition (no AIA on cars)	11,000	
	32,500	
Less: WDA @ 20%	(6,500)	6,500
C/f	26,000	

No adjustment for private use in a company's capital allowances computation.

(2) *Trading profits*

	£
Net profit	429,000
Less: property business income	(4,000)
	425,000
Less: capital allowances (W2)	(6,500)
Trading profits	418,500

(3) *Taxable total profits*

	£
Trading profits	418,500
Property business income	4,000
Taxable total profits	422,500

2

	£
Trading profits	85,000
Interest income £(6,000 + 1,500)	7,500
Chargeable gains	2,950
Less: Gift Aid donation	(15,200)
Taxable total profits	**80,250**

Note. Dividends received do not form part of taxable total profits.

3

	Year to 31 March 2012	3 months ended 30 June 2012
	£	£
Trading profits (12/15 : 3/15)	240,000	60,000
Interest accrued	6,000	1,500
Chargeable gain	250,000	–
Gift Aid	(50,000)	–
Taxable total profits	446,000	61,500

Chapter 10: Computing corporation tax payable

1

	£
Taxable total profits	60,000
Dividends (× 100/90)	5,000
Augmented profits	**65,000**

2

	£
Taxable total profits	2,100,000
Dividend (× 100/90)	50,000
Augmented profits	2,150,000

The main rate of CT applies: £2,100,000 × 26% = **£546,000.00**

Note that although augmented profits are used to work out the rate of tax that applies, CT is only charged on taxable total profits.

3 (1)

	£
Taxable total profits	220,000
Dividends (× 100/90)	100,000
Augmented profits	320,000

Marginal relief applies.

		£
(2)	£220,000 × 26%	57,200.00
	Less: 3/200 $£(1,500,000-320,000)\times\frac{220,000}{320,000}$	(12,168.75)
	CT liability	45,031.25

4

	£
Taxable total profits/augmented profits	60,000

The small profits rate applies.

CT liability £60,000 × 20% = **£12,000.00**

5 (1) Augmented profits are £290,000

This means SPR applies

(2) With a year ended 31 December 2011, 3 months fall into FY10 and 9 months fall into FY11.

(3) Tax on taxable total profits (FY 2010)

£240,000 x 3/12 × 21% =£12,600.00

Tax on taxable total profits (FY 2011)

£240,000 x 9/12 × 20% =£36,000.00

Total CT liability = £12,600 + £36,000 = **£48,600.00**

6 (1)

	£
Taxable total profits	200,000
Dividends (× 100/90)	50,000
Augmented profits	**250,000**

(2) Lower limit

£300,000 × 9/12 = **£225,000**

Upper limit

£1,500,000 × 9/12 = **£1,125,000**

(3) Marginal relief applies:

	£
All of the 9 months fall into FY11	
£200,000 × 26%	52,000.00
$3/200\ £(1{,}125{,}000 - 250{,}000) \times \frac{200{,}000}{250{,}000}$	(10,500.00)
Corporation tax liability	**41,500.00**

Note that the reduced upper limit is used in the marginal relief calculation.

7 (1)

	£
Taxable total profits	360,000
Dividends (× 100/90)	25,000
Augmented profits	**385,000**

(2) Lower limit

£300,000 /3 = **£100,000**

Upper limit

£1,500,000 /3 = **£500,000**

As there are three companies associated with each other, the lower and upper limits are divided by 3.

(3) Marginal relief applies:

FY11	£
£360,000 × 26%	93,600.00
Less: 3/200 $£(500{,}000 - 385{,}000) \times \frac{360{,}000}{385{,}000}$	(1,612.99)
CT liability	**91,987.01**

Chapter 11: Chargeable gains for companies

1

	£
Proceeds of sale	200,000
Cost	(80,000)
Indexation £80,000 × 0.366	(29,280)
Gain	**90,720**

2

	£
Proceeds of sale	20,000
Less: cost	(50,000)
Allowable loss	**(30,000)**

The indexation allowance cannot increase an allowable loss.

3

	£
Proceeds of sale	70,000
Less: cost	(50,000)
Less: indexation allowance 50,000 × 0.624 = 31,200, restricted to £20,000	(20,000)
Gain	**NIL**

The indexation allowance cannot create a loss.

4 (1) The cost of the land being sold is:

$$\frac{400,000}{400,000+600,000} \times £100,000 = \mathbf{£40,000}$$

(2)

	£
Proceeds of sale (net)	391,000
Less: cost	(40,000)
	351,000
Less: indexation allowance £40,000 × 0.324	(12,960)
Chargeable gain	**338,040**

5 False

The horse is a wasting chattel and so there is no chargeable gain on disposal.

6 C

	£
Proceeds of sale	10,000
Less: disposal costs (5% commission)	(500)
Net proceeds of sale	9,500
Less: cost	(2,500)
	7,000
Less: indexation allowance £2,500 x 0.095	(238)
Chargeable gain	6,762
Gain cannot exceed £(10,000 – 6,000) x 5/3	**6,667**

7

	£
Deemed proceeds of sale	6,000
Less: disposal costs £3,600 x 100/90 x 10%	(400)
Net proceeds of sale	5,600
Less: cost	(8,800)
Allowable loss	**(3,200)**

Chapter 12: Share disposals by companies

1 D

1,200 shares acquired on 12 July 2011 (acquisition in previous nine days), then with 800 shares in the FA 1985 pool

2 (1)

	No of shares	Cost	Indexed cost
		£	£
10.8.02 Acquisition	3,000	9,000	9,000
Index to April 2004			
0.041 × £9,000			369
25.4.04 Acquisition	10,000	45,000	45,000
c/f	13,000	54,000	54,369
Index to September 2007			
0.104 × £54,369			5,654
			60,023
13.9.07 Disposal	(1,000)	(4,154)	(4,617)
c/f	12,000	49,846	55,406
Index to November 2011			
0.137 × £55,406			7,591
			62,997
24.11.11 Disposal	(8,500)	(35,308)	(44,623)
c/f	3,500	14,538	18,374

(2)

	£
Proceeds	47,200
Less: cost	(35,308)
	11,892
Less: indexation allowance £(44,623 – 35,308)	(9,315)
Chargeable gain	2,577

3 (1)

		No of shares	Cost	Indexed cost
			£	£
5.01	Acquisition	10,000	45,000	45,000
10.03	Bonus 2:1	20,000		
		30,000		
6.07	Indexed rise			
	£45,000 × 0.163			7,335
	Rights 1:3 @ £4	10,000	40,000	40,000
		40,000	85,000	92,335
1.12	Indexed rise			
	£92,335 × 0.156			14,404
				106,739
	Disposal	(20,000)	(42,500)	(53,370)
		20,000	42,500	53,369

(2)

	£
Proceeds	120,000
Less: cost	(42,500)
	77,500
Less: indexation allowance £(53,370– 42,500)	(10,870)
Chargeable gain	**66,630**

Chapter 13: Corporation tax losses

1 (1)

	£
Trading profits	40,000
Less: carry forward loss relief	(40,000)
	NIL
Property business income	25,000
Chargeable gain	2,000
Taxable total profits	**27,000**

Losses carried forward can be set only against the trading profits. They can not be set against other profits.

(2) Trading losses of **£10,000** (£50,000 – £40,000) remain to be carried forward at 1 April 2012.

2

	Year ended 31 March 2011	**Year ended 31 March 2012**	**Year ended 31 March 2013**
	£	£	£
Trading profits	70,000	NIL	60,000
Less : c/fwd loss relief	-		(60,000)(iii)
Property income	10,000	10,000	10,000
Total profits	80,000	10,000	10,000
Less: CY and C/B loss relief	(80,000)(ii)	(10,000)(i)	
Gift Aid donation	–	–	(10,000)
Taxable total profits	–	–	–
Unrelieved Gift Aid donations	10,000	30,000	5,000

The loss carried forward is £10,000. (£160,000 – £10,000 – £80,000 – £60,000)

3

	Year ended 31 October		
	2009	**2010**	**2011**
	£	**£**	**£**
Trading profits	50,000	40,000	–
Bank interest	10,000	5,000	5,000
Chargeable gain £(12,000 – 7,000)	–	–	5,000
Total profits	60,000	45,000	10,000
Less: current period loss relief	–	–	(10,000)
carry back loss relief	–	(45,000)	–
Taxable total profits	60,000	NIL	NIL

The capital loss has to be carried forward to set against the future chargeable gain. It cannot be set against other profits.

Loss memorandum

	£
Loss	90,000
Less: current period loss relief	(10,000)
	80,000
Less: carry back loss relief (12 months)	(45,000)
Loss to c/f	35,000

Chapter 14: Self assessment for companies

1 The later of:

(a) 30 September 2012, and
(b) 1 September 2012.

ie **30 September 2012.**

2 The two accounting periods are:

(a) **year ended 31 December 2010**, and
(b) **six months to 30 June 2011**.

Tax returns are required for both of these accounting periods. The due date for filing both returns is **30 June 2012.**

3 **£1,000**. The return is more than three but less than six months late so the penalty is £100 plus £10 a day for 90 days. If it had been more than six months late a tax geared penalty would also have been imposed.

4 **31 March 2014** (The return was submitted before the filing due date)

5 **31 January 2013**

6 **B**

As S Ltd is a large company instalments are due as follows:

14 October 2011

14 January 2012

14 April 2012

14 July 2012

ie the final instalment is due on 14 July 2012.

Chapter 15: Chargeable gains for individuals

1

	£
Proceeds of sale	60,000
Less: costs of disposal £(1,200 + 750)	(1,950)
Net proceeds of sale	58,050
Less: original cost	(25,000)
costs of acquisition	(600)
enhancement expenditure	(8,000)
Chargeable gain	24,450

2

	£
Chargeable gains	27,000
Less: annual exempt amount	(10,600)
Taxable gains	16,400

3 D

	£
Chargeable gains	12,000
Less: allowable losses	(1,000)
	11,000
Less: capital losses b/f	(400)
Net gain	10,600

Losses c/f £2,600 £(3,000 – 400)

4

	£
Chargeable gains	38,500
Less: loss	(4,500)
	34,000
Less: Annual exempt amount	(10,600)
Taxable gains	23,400
CGT payable	
£23,400 × 28%	6,552.00

5

	£
Deemed proceeds (market value)	50,000
Less: cost	(60,000)
Allowable loss	(10,000)

The loss may only be set against gains arising on the disposal of other assets by Holly to Emily.

6 A nil

William transfers the asset to his wife Kate on a 'no gain/ no loss' basis. This assumes that William sold it for 'deemed proceeds' equal to his original cost ie £14,000. The market value and the actual proceeds received are not relevant for CGT.

Chapter 16: Share disposal by individuals

1 *Share pool*

	No of shares	*Cost*
		£
5.97 Acquisition	9,000	4,500
8.06 Disposal	(2,000)	(1,000)
c/f	7,000	3,500
5.09 Acquisition	5,000	7,500
	12,000	11,000
1.12 Disposal	(10,000)	(9,167)
c/f	2,000	1,833

Gain	£
Proceeds of sale	20,000
Less: cost	(9,167)
Chargeable gain	10,833

2 Match the disposal first with the same day acquisition:

	£
Proceeds of sale $\frac{1,000}{6,000} \times £21,600$	3,600
Less: cost	(3,800)
Allowable loss	(200)

Then match with the acquisition in the next 30 days:

	£
Proceeds of sale $\frac{500}{6,000} \times £21,600$	1,800
Less: allowable cost	(1,700)
Chargeable gain	100

Finally, match with the share pool:

	£
Proceeds of sale $\frac{4,500}{6,000} \times £21,600$	16,200
Less: allowable cost (W)	(9,643)
Chargeable gain	6,557

The net chargeable gain is therefore:

£(100 + 6,557 – 200)	£6,457

Working

	No of shares	**Cost**
		£
10.8.04 Acquisition	5,000	10,000
15.4.07 Acquisition	2,000	5,000
	7,000	15,000
25.7.11 Disposal	(4,500)	(9,643)
c/f	2,500	5,357

3

	£
Proceeds of sale	18,000
Less: allowable cost (W)	(9,000)
Chargeable gain	9,000

Working

Share pool	**No of shares**	**Cost**
		£
8.02 Acquisition	2,000	10,000
5.05 Rights issue 1 for 1 @ £2.50	2,000	5,000
c/f	4,000	15,000
9.08 Bonus 1 for 4	1,000	0
	5,000	15,000
10.11 Disposal	(3,000)	(9,000)
c/f	2,000	6,000

Chapter 17: Reliefs for chargeable gains

1 The following are qualifying disposals for entrepreneurs' relief:

Part of a business in which the individual has been a partner since August 2009

Unquoted shares held by the individual in a personal trading company in which he is employed and has owned for the previous two years

Quoted shares held by the individual in a personal trading company in which he is employed and has owned for the previous two years

2

	£
Gains eligible for entrepreneurs' relief	50,000
Other gains	33,000
Chargeable gains	83,000
Less: annual exempt amount	(10,600)
Taxable gains	72,400

CGT payable	
£50,000 × 10% (gains eligible for entrepreneurs' relief)	5,000.00
£22,400 × 28% (balance of other gains, no basic rate band remaining unused)	6,272.00
	11,272.00

3 (1)

	No of shares	Cost
		£
May 2002 Acquisition	10,000	50,000
August 2009 Acquisition	1,000	10,000
	11,000	60,000
July 2011 Disposal	(2,200)	(12,000)
c/f	8,800	48,000

(2)

	£
Shares:	
Proceeds of sale	33,500
Less: allowable cost (W)	(12,000)
Gain (eligible for entrepreneurs' relief)	21,500
Painting (not eligible for entrepreneurs' relief)	17,000
Less: loss b/fwd	(1,300)
Less: annual exempt amount	(10,600)
Taxable gain	26,600.00
Shares: £21,500 @ 10%	2,150.00
Painting: £5,100 @ 28%	1,428.00
	3,578.00

4 (1)

	£
Sale proceeds	90,000
Less: cost	(35,000)
Gain	55,000

(2) Gain that can be rolled over is **£55,000** as the amount invested was at least the same as the sale proceeds on disposal of the first factory.

(3) Base cost of new factory £(120,000 – 55,000) = **£65,000**

5 (1) *Offices*

	£
Sale proceeds	100,000
Less: cost	(80,000)
Gain	20,000

(2) Rolled over into factory = **£20,000**

(3) *Factory*

	£	£
Proceeds		375,000
Less: cost	350,000	
Less: rolled over gain	(20,000)	
		(330,000)
Gain		45,000

6 As a replacement factory is purchased in the period commencing one year before and ending three years after the sale of the first factory, rollover relief to defer the gain on the sale of the first factory can be claimed.

Rollover relief is restricted because the full proceeds of sale of the first factory are not reinvested. This means £20,000 of the gain on the first factory is immediately chargeable. The remaining gain of £100,000 is deducted from the base cost of the replacement factory. As a result any gain arising on the future sale of the replacement factory will be larger than it would have been had rollover relief not been claimed.

7 (1)

	£
Proceeds	120,000
Less: cost	(75,000)
	45,000
Less: indexation allowance 0.209 × £75,000	(15,675)
	29,325
Less: rollover relief (balancing figure)	(9,325)
Chargeable gain: amount not reinvested £(120,000 – 100,000)	20,000

(2) The base cost of the workshop is:

	£
Cost of workshop	100,000
Less: rolled over gain	(9,325)
Base cost	90,675

8 (1) *Gift of premises*

	£
Deemed disposal proceeds	400,000
Less: cost	(80,000)
Gain	320,000

Gift relief = **£320,000**

(2) *Sale of premises*

	£	£
Disposal proceeds		675,000
Less: cost	400,000	
Gift relief	(320,000)	
		(80,000)
Gain		595,000

9 Assets qualifying for gift relief are the:

1 Unquoted trading company shares, and the
2 Freehold factory

10 (1) If no gift relief claimed:

Julie's gain

	£
Deemed sale proceeds	85,000
Less: cost	(50,000)
Gain	35,000

Jack's gain

	£
Proceeds	95,000
Less: cost	(85,000)
Gain	10,000

(2) If gift relief claimed:

Julie's gain

	£
Deemed sale proceeds	85,000
Less: cost	(50,000)
	35,000
Less: gift relief	(35,000)
Gain	0

Jack's gain

	£	£
Proceeds		95,000
Less: cost	85,000	
Less: gift relief	(35,000)	
		(50,000)
Gain		45,000

TEST YOUR LEARNING – ANSWERS

Chapter 1: The tax framework

1 **False**

A company pays corporation tax on its total profits

2 **Total income**

3

	Non-savings income	**Savings income**	**Dividend Income**	**Total**
	£	**£**	**£**	**£**
Non-savings income	25,000			
Savings income		12,000		
Dividend income			10,000	
Net income	25,000	12,000	10,000	47,000
Less: personal allowance	(7,475)			(7,475)
Taxable income	17,525	12,000	10,000	39,525

Tax	**£**
Non-savings income	
£17,525 × 20%	3,505.00
Savings income	
£12,000 × 20%	2,400.00
Dividend income	
£5,475 × 10%	547.50
£4,525 × 32.5%	1,470.62
£10,000	**7,923.12**

Chapter 2: Capital allowances

1 **£2,000**

A maximum of the original cost is deducted from the pool.

2 **A**

Year ended 30 June 2011

	AIA	Main pool	Allowances
	£	£	£
B/f		22,500	
Addition qualifying for AIA			
Addition 1.6.11	123,000		
AIA	(100,000)		100,000
	23,000		
Transfer balance to main pool	(23,000)	23,000	
Disposal			
Disposal		(7,800)	
		37,700	
WDA @ 20%		(7,540)	7,540
C/f		30,160	
Allowances			**107,540**

3 *Period ended 31 December 2011*

	FYA @ 100%	Main pool	Allowances
	£	£	£
Addition (no AIA)		18,000	
WDA @ 20% × 6/12		(1,800)	1,800
		16,200	
Addition	5,000		
FYA @ 100%	(5,000)		5,000
C/f		16,200	
			6,800

Note. The AIA and WDAs are time apportioned in a short period. FYAs are not. AIAs and FYAs are not available on a car with CO_2 emissions of 145g/km.

4 **False**

There is no AIA or WDA in the final period so a balancing allowance arises as follows:

	£
B/f	12,500
Addition	20,000
Proceeds	(18,300)
	14,200
Balancing allowance	(14,200)

5 *Year ended 30 April 2012*

	Private use asset @ 60%	**Allowances**
	£	**£**
Addition	30,000	
WDA @ 10%	(3,000) × 60%	1,800
C/f	27,000	

6 **B**

Lower of £19,000 @ 20% (£3,800) and £3,000 ie £3,000. CO_2 emissions not relevant for cars acquired before 6 April 2009.

Chapter 3: Computing trading income

1 **B** and **C**

Legal fees on the acquisition of factory are capital expenditure and so not allowable. Heating is a revenue expense and so allowable. Legal fees incurred on pursuing trade receivables are allowable as they relate to a revenue source. Acquiring a machine is a capital expense and so not allowable (although capital allowances will be available for this expenditure).

2 £700.

The cost of staff entertaining is allowable.

Gifts of food are never allowable. The entertaining of customers is never allowable.

3

	Allowable	**Disallowable**
Parking fines incurred by the owner of the business		✓
Parking fines incurred by an employee whilst on the employer's business	✓	
Legal costs incurred in relation to acquiring a 10 year lease of property for the first time		✓
Legal costs incurred in relation to the renewal of a lease for 20 years	✓	
Gifts of calendars to customers, costing £4 each and displaying an advertisement for the trade concerned	✓	
Gifts of bottles of whisky to customers, costing £12 each		✓

4 **D**

The normal selling price of £80 + (20% × £80) = £96 must be added to the accounts profit.

5 The movement on the general provision is disallowable (if an increase)/not taxable (if a decrease). This means that the decrease in the general provision of **£700** (£2,500 – £1,800) must be deducted from the accounts profit.

6 80% × £450 = **£360** is disallowable for tax purposes.

Chapter 4: Taxing unincorporated businesses

1

Tax year	Basis period
2011/12	1 May 2011 – 5 April 2012
2012/13	Year ended 31 December 2012
2013/14	Year ended 31 December 2013
Overlap profits	1 January 2012 – 5 April 2012

2 **True**

When the trade ceases overlap profits are deducted from the final year's taxable profits.

3

Tax year	Basis period	Taxable profits £
2009/10	1 June 2008 to 31 May 2009	£18,000
2010/11	1 June 2009 to 31 May 2010	£32,000
2011/12	1 June 2010 – 31 December 2011	£30,000

In 2011/12, taxable profits are (£25,000 + £15,000 – £10,000) = £30,000

4 2010/11 (1 February 2011 – 5 April 2011)
£34,000 × 2/17 = £4,000

2011/12 (6 April 2011 – 5 April 2012)
£34,000 × 12/17 = £24,000

2012/13 (12 months ended 30 June 2012)
£34,000 × 12/17 = £24,000

Overlap profits (1 July 2011 to 5 April 2012)
9/17 × £34,000 = **£18,000**

5 (1)

2010/11 (1 December 2010 – 5 April 2011)
4/7 × £70,000 = **£40,000**

(2)

2011/12 (1 December 2010 – 30 November 2011)
£70,000 + 5/12 × £60,000 = **£95,000**

(3)

2012/13 (1 July 2011 to 30 June 2012) **£60,000**

(4)

Overlap profits

	£
1 December 2010 – 5 April 2011	40,000
1 July 2011 – 30 November 2011	25,000
	65,000

Chapter 5: Partnerships

1 C

The period of account concerned.

2

	Total	Dave	Joe
	£	£	£
1.1.11 – 30.9.11(9/12)	13,500	6,750	6,750
1.10.11 – 31.12.11 (3/12)	4,500	2,700	1,800
	18,000	9,450	8,550

Dave has taxable profits of **£9,450** for 2011/12 and Joe has taxable profits of **£8,550** for 2011/12.

3

	Total	Sunita	Jasmine
	£	£	£
Salary	85,000	5,000	80,000
Profits (£200,000 – £85,000)	115,000	57,500	57,500
	200,000	62,500	137,500

4 **D**

2011/12 (year ended 31 March 2012)

Taxable profits on Steve for 2011/12 are £20,000 (1/4 × £80,000).

5 Year ended 31 August 2012

	Total	Abdul	Ghita	Sase
	£	£	£	£
Profits (2:2:1)	120,000	48,000	48,000	24,000

The opening year rules apply to Sase.

2011/12 (1 September 2011 – 5 April 2012)

7/12 × £24,000 = **£14,000**

2012/13 (year ended 31 August 2012) = **£24,000**

Overlap profits = **£14,000**

6 (1)

	Total	**William**	**Ann**	**John**
	£	**£**	**£**	**£**
Y/e 31.10.10	21,000	7,000	7,000	7,000
Y/e 31.10.11	33,000	11,000	11,000	11,000
Y/e 31.10.12				
1.11.11 – 31.12.11 (2/12)	6,000	2,000	2,000	2,000
1.1.12 – 31.10.12 (10/12)	30,000	–	15,000	15,000
	36,000	2,000	17,000	17,000

(2)

	Ann	**John**	**William**
	£	**£**	**£**
2010/11 (y/e 31 October 2010)	7,000	7,000	7,000
2011/12 (y/e 31 October 2011)	11,000	11,000	8,000
2012/13 (y/e 31 October 2012)	17,000	17,000	0

Ann and John will be taxed on the current year basis of assessment throughout. The cessation rules apply to William in 2011/12, the year he left the business:

1 November 2010 – 31 December 2011 (£11,000 + £2,000 – £5,000) = £8,000

Chapter 6: Losses

1 **D**

2011/12 and/or 2010/11

2 **False**

Trading losses can be carried forward indefinitely.

3 **C**

Against trading income arising in the same trade

4 The loss is a loss of 2011/12.

It can be:

(a) Deducted from total income of £9,000 in 2011/12 and/or from total income of £19,000 in 2010/11.

(b) Carried forward to be deducted from taxable trading profits of £25,000 in 2012/13 and then in later years.

Chapter 7: National insurance

1 No Class 2 NICs as earnings below small earnings exception

No Class 4 NICs due as profits below annual lower profits limit of £7,225

Total NICs **£0.00**

2

		£
Class 2 NICs	52 × £2.50	130.00
Class 4 NICs	(£42,475 – £7,225) × 9%	3,172.50
	(£50,000 – £42,475) × 2%	150.50
Total NICs		**3,453.00**

3 Class 2 NICs 52 × £2.50 = **£130.00**

Class 4 NICs (£10,850 – £7,225) × 9% = **£326.25**

Total NICs = **£456.25**

Chapter 8: Self assessment for individuals

1 **31 January 2013**

2 Payments on account of income tax for 2011/12 are due on:

31 January 2012 and 31 July 2012

Each payment on account due is equal to 50% of the prior year's (2010/11) income tax payable

3 £100 penalty for failure to deliver return on time.

Possible £10 per day penalty from 1 May 2013 until date of filing.

5% penalty on tax paid late. Interest on tax paid late.

4 **D**

28 January 2014. A year after the actual filing date because Susie filed the return before the due filing date (31 January 2013).

5 £6,000 31 January 2012

£6,000 31 July 2012

£4,000 31 January 2013

6 **£0**

No penalties for late payment are due on late payments on account.

7 The maximum penalty that could be imposed on Lola is:

C £1,020

ie 30% × PLR

PLR = £17,000 × 20% = £3,400

Chapter 9: Computing taxable total profits

1

	Type of income	Amount received	Amount to be included
(1)	building society interest	£6,000	**£6,000**
(2)	bank deposit interest	£3,900	**£3,900**
(3)	dividends from other companies	£9,000	**£0**
(4)	patent royalties received from an individual (x 100/80)	£6,000	**£7,500**

2 **C**

Deducted to compute trading income (loan is for trading purposes)

3 **£385**

Companies make gross Gift Aid donations.

4 **B**

The first accounting period is always 12 months in length in a long accounting period.

5

	Year ended 31.12.11	4 months ended 30.4.12
	£	£
Trading profits (12/16 : 4/16)	240,000	80,000
Interest (accrued for each period)	1,200	400
Gain (allocate to period made)	0	20,000
Less: Gift Aid (allocate to period paid)	(15,000)	–
Taxable total profits	226,200	100,400

Chapter 10: Computing corporation tax payable

1 C

	£
Taxable total profits	255,000
Dividend	–
Augmented profits	255,000

Lower limit £300,000 × 6/12 = £150,000

Upper limit £1,500,000 × 6/12 = £750,000

As this is a six month period, the limits are multiplied by 6/12.

Marginal relief applies:

FY11

	£
£255,000 × 26%	66,300.00
Less: 3/200 £(750,000 – 255,000)	(7,425)
	58,875.00

2 Augmented profits = £55,000

Lower limit £300,000 × 9/12 = £225,000

Small profits rate applies:

FY11

£50,000 × 20% = **£10,000.00**

3 1) Augmented profits are £90,000

This means SPR applies

2) With a year ended 31 December 2011, 3 months fall into FY10 and 9 months fall into FY11.

3)

Tax on taxable total profits (FY 2010)

£90,000 × 3/12 × 21% =£4,725.00

Tax on taxable total profits (FY 2011)

£90,000 × 9/12 × 20% =£13,500.00

Total CT liability = £4,725 + £13,500 = **£18,225.00**

4 C

Taxable total profits = £180,000

Lower limit £300,000/2 × 9/12 = £112,500

Upper limit £1,500,000/2 × 9/12 = £562,500

There are two associated companies, so the limits are divided by 2. The limits are also multiplied by 9/12 as this is a short accounting period.

Marginal relief applies:

	£
FY11	
£180,000 × 26%	46,800.00
Less: 3/200 £(562,500 – 180,000)	(5,737.50)
	41,062.50

5 D

27.5%

6 True

Financial Year 2011 begins on 1 April 2011 and ends on 31 March 2012.

Chapter 11: Chargeable gains for companies

1 Indexation allowance runs **from the date the expenditure was incurred** to **the date of disposal.**

2

	£
Proceeds of sale	200,000
Less: cost	(80,000)
Less: enhancement expenditure	(10,000)
	110,000
Less: indexation allowance on cost £80,000 × 0.301	(24,080)
Less: indexation allowance on enhancement £10,000 × 0.214	(2,140)
Chargeable gain	83,780

3 (1) The cost of the land being sold is:

$$\frac{80,000}{80,000 + 120,000} \times £50,000 = £20,000$$

(2)

	£
Proceeds of sale	80,000
Less: cost	(20,000)
	60,000
Less: indexation allowance £20,000 × 0.188	(3,760)
Chargeable gain	**56,240**

4

	£
Proceeds of sale	8,000
Less: cost	(3,500)
	4,500
Less: indexation allowance £3,500 × 0.045	(158)
Chargeable gain	4,342
Gain cannot exceed £(8,000 – 6,000) × 5/3	**3,333**

5 C

	£
Deemed proceeds of sale	6,000
Less: cost	(8,700)
Allowable loss	**(2,700)**

Chapter 12: Share disposals by companies

1 The matching rules for shares disposed of by a company shareholder are:

(a) Shares acquired on the same day
(b) Shares acquired in the previous nine days (FIFO)
(c) Shares from the FA 1985 pool

2 (1)

		No of shares	Cost	Indexed cost
			£	£
5.01	Acquisition	10,000	90,000	90,000
6.07	Indexed rise			
	£90,000 × 0.163			14,670
	Rights 1:4 @ £12	2,500	30,000	30,000
		12,500	120,000	134,670
1.12	Indexed rise			
	£134,670 × 0.156			21,009
				155,679
	Disposal	(10,000)	(96,000)	(124,543)
		2,500	24,000	31,136

(2)

	£
Proceeds	150,000
Less: cost	(96,000)
	54,000
Less: indexation allowance £(124,543 – 96,000)	(28,543)
Chargeable gain	25,457

Chapter 13: Corporation tax losses

1 (1)

	Year ended 31 October	
	2010	**2011**
	£	**£**
Trading profit	170,000	–
Interest	5,000	60,000
Capital gain £(12,000 – 20,000)	–	–
Total profits	175,000	60,000
Less: current period loss relief		(60,000)
Less: carry back loss relief	(175,000)	
Less: Gift Aid	–	–
	NIL	NIL
Unrelieved Gift Aid donations	5,000	5,000

Trade losses of **£85,000** (£320,000 – £60,000 – £175,000) remain to be carried forward at 1 November 2011.

(2) A capital loss of **£8,000** (£20,000 – £12,000) remains to be carried forward at 1 November 2011.

2 B

	Year ended 31.3.10	Six months 30.9.10	Year ended 30.9.11
	£	**£**	**£**
Trading profit	4,000	6,000	–
Less: current period loss relief	–	–	–
carry back loss relief	(2,000)	(6,000)	–
Gift Aid	–	–	–
Taxable total profits	–	–	–

The maximum relief for year ended 31.3.10 is £4,000 × 6/12 = £2,000.

Chapter 14: Self assessment for companies

1. By **1 June 2013** (12 months after the actual filing date).

2. **£100** (The return is less than 3 months late).

3. **B**

   1 October 2012. Girton Ltd is a small company, so all CT is due nine months after the end of the accounting period.

4. **C**

   14 July 2012. Eaton Ltd is a large company and is required to pay corporation tax by instalments. The first instalment is due in the seventh month of the accounting period.

5. 1/4 × £240,000 = **£60,000**

Chapter 15: Chargeable gains for individuals

1

	£
Proceeds	560,000
Less: cost	(325,000)
Chargeable gain	**235,000**

2 **A**

	£
Proceeds	38,000
Less: costs of disposal	(3,000)
Less: £41,500 × $\frac{38,000}{38,000+48,000}$	(18,337)
Chargeable gain	**16,663**

3

	£
Gains	171,000
Less: current year losses	(5,300)
	165,700
Less: losses b/f	(10,000)
	155,700
Less: annual exempt amount	(10,600)
Taxable gains	**145,100**

There are no losses to carry forward.

4

	£
Chargeable gains	23,800
Less: annual exempt amount	(10,600)
Taxable gains	13,200
CGT on £13,200 @ 28%	**3,696**

5 **31 January 2013**

6 (a) There is no gain or loss as the chattel is sold for gross proceeds of less than £6,000.

(b)

	£
Net proceeds	8,200
Less: cost	(3,500)
	4,700

Gain cannot exceed 5/3 (8,420 – 6,000) = £4,033

Therefore, gain is **£4,033.**

7 £0.

A racehorse is an exempt asset, so no chargeable gain or allowable loss arises.

8

	£
Deemed proceeds	6,000
Less: cost	(7,000)
Allowable loss	**(1,000)**

9 False

A loss on a disposal to a connected person can be set only against gains arising on disposals to the same connected person.

10 True

No gain or loss arises on a disposal to a spouse/civil partner.

11

	Actual proceeds used	Deemed proceeds (market value) used	No gain or loss basis
Paul sells an asset to his civil partner Joe for £3,600			✓
Grandmother gives an asset to grandchild worth £1,000		✓	
Sarah sells an asset to best friend Cathy for £12,000 worth £20,000		✓	

Chapter 16: Share disposal by individuals

1 **D**

	No of shares	Cost
		£
8.92 Acquisition	10,000	5,000
4.07 Acquisition	10,000	16,000
	20,000	21,000
11.10 Disposal	(15,000)	(15,750)
c/f	5,000	5,250

	£
Proceeds of sale	30,000
Less: allowable cost	(15,750)
Chargeable gain	**14,250**

2 False.

In a rights issue shares are paid for and this amount is added to the original cost. In a bonus issue shares are not paid for and so there is no adjustment to the original cost.

3

	No of shares	Cost
		£
5.01 Acquisition	2,000	12,000
12.02 1 for 2 rights issue @ £7.50	1,000	7,500
	3,000	19,500
3.12 Disposal	(2,500)	(16,250)
c/f	500	3,250

	£
Proceeds of sale	20,000
Less: allowable costs	(16,250)
Chargeable gain	**3,750**

Chapter 17: Reliefs for chargeable gains

1

	£
Gains	10,400,000
Less: annual exempt amount	(10,600)
Chargeable gain	10,389,400
CGT:	
10,000,000 @ 10%	1,000,000.00
389,400 @ 28%	109,032.00
	1,109,032.00

2

	£
Proceeds of sale	80,000
Less: allowable cost	(10,000)
Taxable gain (no annual exempt amount available)	70,000
CGT @ 10%	7,000.00

3 **B**

The office block and the freehold warehouse were acquired outside the qualifying reinvestment period commencing one year before and ending three years after the disposal.

The fork lift truck is not fixed plant and machinery.

4 **C**

Land

	£
Sales proceeds	400,000
Less: cost	(100,000)
Gain	300,000

£20,000 of the proceeds are not reinvested, so £20,000 of the gain remains chargeable, £280,000 is rolled over.

Replacement land

	£	£
Sale proceeds		500,000
Less: cost	380,000	
Rolled over gain	(280,000)	
		(100,000)
Chargeable gain		400,000

5 **True**

6 If relief for replacement of business assets is to be claimed, a new asset must be acquired between **16 January 2011** and **14 January 2015**.

7 The gain on the sale of first warehouse is:

	£
Proceeds	400,000
Less: cost	(220,000)
	180,000
Less: indexation allowance	(40,000)
	140,000
Less: rollover relief (balancing figure)	(115,000)
Chargeable gain: amount not reinvested £(400,000 – 375,000)	**25,000**

8 **False**

Jewellery is not a qualifying asset for gift relief purposes.

9 *Gift*

	£
Market value	200,000
Less: cost	(50,000)
Gain	150,000
Less: gift relief	(150,000)
Gain left in charge	**0**

Sale

	£
Sale proceeds	350,000
Less: cost (£200,000 – £150,000)	(50,000)
Gain	**300,000**

INDEX

Accounting period, 111
Allowable costs, 135
Annual exempt amount, 179
Annual investment allowance, 12
Associated company, 125

Badges of trade, 32
Balancing payment, 98
Basis period, 50
Bonus issue, 152, 190

Capital allowances, 10
Capital expenditure, 10, 34
Capital gains tax, 180
Capital losses
  Companies, 162
  Individuals, 179
Carry back loss relief, 160
Carry forward loss relief, 158
Cessation of trading, 54
Chargeable asset, 134
Chargeable disposal, 134
Chargeable gains
  Companies, 108, 134
  Individuals, 178
Chargeable person, 134
Charitable donations, 37
Chattels, 139, 181
Company, 2
Company tax return, 128
Connected persons, 182
Corporation tax, 119
Current period loss relief, 159
Current year basis of assessment, 50

Depooling election, 23
Disallowable expenditure, 35
Disposal consideration, 135

Enhancement expenditure, 135
Enquiries, 170
Enquiries, 100
Entrepreneurs' relief, 196
Expensive cars, 24

FA 1985 pool, 148
Filing due date
  Companies, 168
  Individuals, 92
Finance Act, 2
Financial year, 118
First year allowance 100%, 13
Fiscal year, 50

Gift aid donations, 108
Gift relief, 206

HMRC, 2

Incidental costs of disposal, 135
Indexation allowance, 136
Instalments, 171
Interest on late paid tax, 99, 172
Interest on over paid tax, 100, 172
Interest paid by companies, 108
Interest received by companies, 108

Large companies, 171

Main pool, 11
Marginal rate of tax, 127
Matching rules
  Companies, 146
  Individuals, 188

National insurance contributions, 86
Net income, 3
No gain/no loss disposals, 182
Notification of chargeability
  Companies, 168
  Individuals, 92

Opening year rules, 50
Operative events, 148
Overlap profits, 55

Part disposals, 178
Part disposals, 138
Partnership, 2, 64
Payment of capital gains tax, 181
Payment of corporation tax, 171, 173
Payment of income tax, 97
Payment on account, 97
Penalties for error, 94, 170
Penalties for failure to keep records, 96, 169
Penalties for late filing
  Individuals, 96
Penalties for late notification, 95, 168
Penalties for late payment of tax, 98
Period of account, 12, 111
Plant, 10
Private use asset, 22
Profits, 118
Profits chargeable to corporation tax, 106
Profits., 106
Property business income, 108
Property business losses, 163

Records
  Companies, 169
  Individuals, 93

Revenue expenditure, 10, 34
Rights issue, 152, 191
Rollover relief, 203

Self employment tax return pages, 57
Short life asset, 23
Small companies' marginal relief, 120
Small Profits Rate, 121
Sole trader, 2
Special rate pool, 21
Spouses/civil partners, 182

Tax year, 50
Taxable gains, 178
Taxable income, 3
Total income, 3
Trading losses
  Companies, 158
  Individuals, 80
Trading profits
  companies, 106
  individuals, 35

Wasting chattel, 139
Wholly and exclusively for trade purposes, 36
Writing down allowance, 14

Year of assessment, 50

REVIEW FORM

How have you used this Text?
(Tick one box only)

☐ Home study

☐ On a course ____________________

☐ Other ____________________

Why did you decide to purchase this Text?
(Tick one box only)

☐ Have used BPP Texts in the past

☐ Recommendation by friend/colleague

☐ Recommendation by a college lecturer

☐ Saw advertising

☐ Other ____________________

During the past six months do you recall seeing/receiving either of the following?
(Tick as many boxes as are relevant)

☐ Our advertisement in Accounting Technician

☐ Our Publishing Catalogue

Which (if any) aspects of our advertising do you think are useful?
(Tick as many boxes as are relevant)

☐ Prices and publication dates of new editions

☐ Information on Text content

☐ Details of our free online offering

☐ None of the above

Your ratings, comments and suggestions would be appreciated on the following areas of this Text.

	Very useful	*Useful*	*Not useful*
Introductory section	☐	☐	☐
Quality of explanations	☐	☐	☐
How it works	☐	☐	☐
Chapter tasks	☐	☐	☐
Chapter Overviews	☐	☐	☐
Test your learning	☐	☐	☐
Index	☐	☐	☐

	Excellent	*Good*	*Adequate*	*Poor*
Overall opinion of this Text	☐	☐	☐	☐

Do you intend to continue using BPP Products? ☐ Yes ☐ No

Please note any further comments and suggestions/errors on the reverse of this page. The publishing manager of this edition can be e-mailed at: ambercottrell@bpp.com

Please return to: Amber Cottrell, Publishing Manager, BPP Learning Media Ltd, FREEPOST, London, W12 8BR.

REVIEW FORM (continued)

TELL US WHAT YOU THINK

Please note any further comments and suggestions/errors below.